Busy in the Bible

Jonah 1
Amplified Bible Study

Paula Nafziger

Large Print 16 point

King James Today™

Title .... Busy in the Bible Jonah 1
Subtitle........... Amplified Bible Study
Print................. Large Print — 16 point
Bible Version... King James Today™
Author .... Paula Nafziger, Chaplain
ISBN-13 978-1-639-42045-2

9 8 7 6 5 4 3 2 1

Cover—Whale shark and scuba diver

Table of Contents

1 1 Now the word of the Lord came to
Jonah the son of Amittai, saying,
2 *Arise, go to Nineveh, that great city, and cry against*
it; for their wickedness is come up before me.
3 But Jonah rose up to flee to Tarshish from the presence
of the Lord, and went down to Joppa;
and he found a ship going to Tarshish: so he paid
the fare thereof, and went down into it, to go with
them to Tarshish from the presence of the Lord.
4 But the Lord sent out a great wind into the
sea, and there was a mighty tempest in the sea,
so that the ship was like to be broken.
5 Then the mariners were afraid, and cried every man to
his god, and cast forth the wares that were in the ship into
the sea, to lighten it of them. But Jonah was gone down
into the sides of the ship; and he lay, and was fast asleep.
6 So the shipmaster came to him, and said to him, What
mean you, O sleeper? arise, call upon your God, if so

Key: Direct words of God (or quoted by His messengers) appear in italic.

be that God will think upon us, that we perish not.

7 And they said every one to his fellow, Come, and let us
cast lots, that we may know for whose cause this evil is
upon us. So they cast lots, and the lot fell upon Jonah.

8 Then said they to him, Tell us, we pray you
for whose cause this evil is upon us; What is
your occupation? and where come you? what is
your country? and of what people are you?

9 And he said to them, I am a Hebrew; and
I fear the Lord, the God of heaven, which
has made the sea and the dry land.

10 Then were the men exceedingly afraid, and said to him.
Why have you done this? For the men knew that he fled
from the presence of the Lord, because he had told them.

11 Then said they to him, What shall we do to
you that the sea may be calm to us? for the
sea wrought, and was tempestuous.

12 And he said to them, Take me up, and cast me forth
into the sea; so shall the sea be calm to you: for I know
that for my sake this great tempest is upon you.

13 Nevertheless the men rowed hard to bring
it to the land; but they could not: for the sea
wrought, and was tempestuous against them.

14 Wherefore they cried to the Lord, and said, We
beseech you O Lord, we beseech you let us not perish
for this man's life, and lay not upon us innocent blood:
for you, O Lord, have done as it pleased you.

15 So they took up Jonah, and cast him forth into
the sea: and the sea ceased from her raging.

16 Then the men feared the Lord exceedingly, and
offered a sacrifice to the Lord, and made vows.

17 Now the Lord had prepared a great fish to
swallow up Jonah. And Jonah was in the belly
of the fish three days and three nights.

JONAH

2 1 Then Jonah prayed to the Lord his
God out of the fish's belly,
2 And said, I cried by reason of my affliction
to the Lord, and he heard me; out of the belly
of hell cried I, and you heard my voice.
3 For you had cast me into the deep, in the midst of
the seas; and the floods compassed me about: all
your billows and your waves passed over me.
4 Then I said, I am cast out of your sight; yet I
will look again toward your holy temple.
5 The waters compassed me about, even to
the soul: the depth closed me round about,
the weeds were wrapped about my head.
6 I went down to the bottoms of the mountains; the
earth with her bars was about me forever: yet have you
brought up my life from corruption, O Lord my God.
7 When my soul fainted within me I remembered the Lord:
and my prayer came in to you into your holy temple.

8 They that observe lying vanities forsake their own mercy.

9 But I will sacrifice to you with the voice of thanksgiving;
I will pay that that I have vowed. Salvation is of the Lord.

10 And the Lord spoke to the fish, and it
vomited out Jonah upon the dry land.

3

1 And the word of the Lord came to
Jonah the second time, saying,
2 *Arise, go to Nineveh, that great city, and
preach to it the preaching that I bid you.*
3 So Jonah arose, and went to Nineveh, according
to the word of the Lord. Now Nineveh was an
exceeding great city of three days' journey.
4 And Jonah began to enter into the city a
day's journey, and he cried, and said, Yet forty
days, and Nineveh shall be overthrown.
5 So the people of Nineveh believed God, and
proclaimed a fast, and put on sackcloth, from the
greatest of them even to the least of them.
6 For word came to the king of Nineveh, and he arose
from his throne, and he laid his robe from him, and
covered him with sackcloth, and sat in ashes.
7 And he caused it to be proclaimed and published
through Nineveh by the decree of the king and his

nobles, saying, Let neither man nor beast, herd nor flock,
taste any thing: let them not feed, nor drink water:
8 But let man and beast be covered with sackcloth, and
cry mightily to God: yea, let them turn every one from his
evil way, and from the violence that is in their hands.
9 Who can tell if God will turn and repent, and turn
away from his fierce anger, that we perish not?
10 And God saw their works, that they turned from
their evil way; and God repented of the evil, that he
had said that he would do to them; and he did it not.

4 1 But it displeased Jonah exceedingly,
and he was very angry.
2 And he prayed to the Lord, and said, I pray you O Lord,
was not this my saying, when I was yet in my country?
Therefore I fled before to Tarshish: for I knew that
you are a gracious God, and merciful, slow to anger,
and of great kindness, and repent you of the evil.
3 Therefore now, O Lord, take, I beseech you my life
from me; for it is better for me to die than to live.
4 Then said the Lord, *Do you well to be angry?*
5 So Jonah went out of the city, and sat on the east side of
the city, and there made him a booth, and sat under it in the
shadow, till he might see what would become of the city.
6 And the Lord God prepared a gourd, and made it
to come up over Jonah, that it might be a shadow
over his head, to deliver him from his grief. So
Jonah was exceeding glad of the gourd.

7 But God prepared a worm when the morning rose
the next day, and it smote the gourd that it withered.

8 And it came to pass, when the sun did arise, that God
prepared a vehement east wind; and the sun beat upon
the head of Jonah, that he fainted, and wished in himself
to die, and said, It is better for me to die than to live.

9 And God said to Jonah, *Do you well to be angry for the*
gourd? And he said, I do well to be angry, even to death.

10 Then said the Lord, *You have had pity on the gourd,*
for the which you have not labored, neither made it grow;
which came up in a night, and perished in a night:

11 *And should not I spare Nineveh, that great*
city, wherein are more than sixscore thousand
persons that cannot discern between their right
hand and their left hand; and also much cattle?

Go? Nah!

Have you ever felt God wanted you to do or say something, but instead of "yes," your response or attitude was "Nah!" That's how the Book of Jonah begins. God said *Go*—Jonah said *No!*

What happens when a man or woman "of God" refuses God's directive? Can we hide from His sight? Who's in control, He or we?

The Old Testament story of Jonah is well-known. The word ***story*** can be misunderstood. It has several possible meanings depending on the communicator's intent. It can refer to:

1. A verbal or written narration or recital of events, facts, or incidents.
2. History: a written narrative or account of past transactions relating to nations or individuals.

But the word *story* can also refer to:

3. A petty or trifling tale; talking without seriousness.
4. A fiction or fable.
5. A softer term for a lie.

It isn't wrong to call the Biblical account of Jonah a "story," but you'll need to decide what is meant by the word "story."

So far, *in my opinion*, the Book of Jonah, or story of Jonah, is:

Fiction, fake, and a fabrication of one's mind. ❍Agree ❍Disagree ❍?

A true **non-fiction** narrative of ancient history. ❍Agree ❍Disagree ❍?

Record the date you start this study here:

 Date: ________

Fiction means:

1. An idea or conception of something *not* factual, true, or real.
2. Something fabricated or invented.
3. A notion or idea in the mind, known as imagery or imagination.

Memory aid: ***Fiction** is **Fake***

Stories classified as fiction include:

Fable:

1. A **feigned** [invented; devised; imagined; assumed] story intended to amuse and/or instruct.
2. A **fictitious** [not real] narration intended to enforce a truth or **precept** [commandment or order intended as an authoritative rule of action].
2. An **idle** [an invention, falsehood] story (which 1 Timothy 4:7 teaches to refuse).
3. **Falsehood** [contrary to or in conformity to fact or truth]. The word falsehood is a softer term for a lie.
4. A short story intended to teach a **moral** [in reference to right and wrong] lesson, typically with animals or **inanimate** [not having animation or life] objects as characters.

Fairy tale:

1. A fictitious, unrealistic story, usually told to amuse children.
2. A made-up, non-credible story often involving magical or mythical creatures in **implausible** [not wearing the appearance of truth or credibility, and not likely to be believed] events and situations.

Folklore:

1. An unsupported notion, saying, or story.
2. Oral communication of beliefs, customs, myths, practices, tales, and ways preserved of particular groups of people.

Legend:

1. An idle or ridiculous story told respecting saints.
2. An incredible, unauthentic narrative.
3. An unverified story from the past, especially one popularly believed to be historical.

Myth:

1. A traditional story, told *as if it were* factual, usually about the early history of a people.
2. A false belief based on **delusion** [error or mistake proceeding from false views] or **fantasy** [produced or existing only in imagination; unrestrained fancy].

Tale:

1. A story, fictitious narrative; the rehearsal of a series of events or adventures, commonly of **trifling** [not important, of small value] incidents.
2. A narrative of **imaginary** [existing only in imagination or fancy, not real] events told as though **real** [actually being or existing, true; genuine; not artificial or counterfeit].

Non-Fiction means:

Written or spoken language based on real/actual events, evidence, facts, real people, and truth, which can apply to academic texts, biographies, commentary, history, instructional manuals, journalism, travelogues, etc.

Memory aid: ***NON-Fiction*** *is* ***NOT Fake***

A famous example of one story is found in Aesop's Fables 1547 A.D., "The Hare and the Tortoise," also known in modern times as The Tortoise and the Hare.

The Hare (an animal similar to a rabbit) is distinguished by its tall ears and long, powerful hind legs (that can run up to 48 miles/77 km per hour.) The fastest speed recorded for a tortoise is .62 mph (less than one mph/km).

The Tortoise and the Hare

> A Hare was one-day making fun of a Tortoise for being so slow upon his feet. "Wait a bit," said the Tortoise; "I'll run a race with you, and I'll wager that I win." "Oh, well," replied the Hare, who was much amused at the idea, "let's try and see," and it was soon agreed that the fox should set a course for them and be the judge. When the time came, both started off together, but the Hare was soon so far ahead that he thought he might as well have a rest, so down he lay and fell fast asleep. Meanwhile, the Tortoise kept plodding on and, in time, reached the goal. At last, the Hare woke up with a start and dashed on at his fastest, only to find that the Tortoise had already won the race.

The story of The Tortoise and the Hare is:

Fiction—❍ Fable ❍ Fairy tale ❍ Folklore ❍ Legend ❍ Myth ❍ Tale

Non-Fiction—❍ A narration of events, facts, and incidents.
❍ A historical record of past transactions.

What lesson or wisdom can you extract from the story of The Tortoise and the Hare?

How could the above apply to your personal Bible study habits:

Since the story of Jonah involves an animal/marine mammal/great fish, is it *possible* the story is a fable (fiction/fake)? ... ❍Yes ❍No ❍?

By **plodding** [traveling or working slowly or with steady laborious diligence] through this study and paying attention to details, you'll be able to articulate and defend your judgment or opinion on the story of Jonah. You'll grow in confidence in what you believe *and why!*

The Book of Jonah contains only four chapters. This study focuses on Chapter 1 only, in great detail, because God is in the details!

Turn the page, and let's get started!

pray
MORE
Worry
LESS

Welcome!

I am so glad you have decided to study God's word!

We will begin with an understanding of prayer.

What Is Prayer?

Prayer is simply "talking to God." You can communicate verbally (outloud), silently in your heart (thoughts of your mind), or through writing (prayer on paper). Relationships are built upon communication, and for Believers, praying should be as common as thinking. Even though God knows your heart, He wants you to sincerely communicate your concerns, desires, emotions, feelings, needs, thoughts, and words in God-honoring ways, seasoned with humility.

There are many reasons to pray, including your need for wisdom, guidance, strength to resist temptation, and the Holy Spirit's intervention to fight Spiritual battles. Prayer is a personal and unique experience. There are no rules, no set order, and no specific words or positions required. You can pray in your own language, in your own way, anytime and anywhere. Your prayer doesn't need to be spoken in antiquated languages, words, or dialects (such as King James Old English) or shouted as though God cannot hear, nor does it need to sound or appear "religious." *Sincerity of heart is the goal in communication with God.*

While prayer can be a time to support and encourage others, it should not be used to show off, draw attention to yourself, criticize, spread rumors, fuel gossip, etc. God wants intimate communication with you—not a passionless repetition of words. *What you mean matters more than what you say.* He hears and communicates back in unique ways, often using His word as you read and study it.

Pray & Read

Begin your Bible study time by talking to God. Then, if you remain silent for a few moments afterward, God might prompt your heart/mind with something He wants you to hear or know.

Take a moment to write a prayer of what you **hope** [the expectation of good] God does through this Bible study.

▲ *Note: This workbook does not provide complete education on Biblical word study. The definitions are not an exhaustive list of available choices and require human interpretation. Avoid taking a hard stance on the exact meaning of words based on this book alone. It should get you close, but not close enough without further research.*

1❍ Take *five to ten minutes* to read through the entire Book of Jonah in one sitting, *all four chapters*. When you finish, fill in the bubble if you like to track your progress.

2❍ Who is the author/writer of the Book of Jonah?
❍ Amittai ❍ Anonymous ❍ Jonah ❍ Joshua ❍ Mariner/Sailor
❍ Moses ❍ Nineveh ❍ Priests ❍ Scribes ❍ Unknown ❍ Other

If you like to write or journal, use the space below to record any thoughts you have:

You might wonder if there is anything in the Book of Jonah relevant for today or that you could apply to your personal circumstances.

To get an overview of the book, you'll spend the next few days reading one chapter a day and then answer a few questions.

Congratulations, you finished. Keep up the good habit!

Observe—Chapter 1

1❑ Take *3 to 4 minutes* to read all 17 verses of Jonah **Chapter 1**.

2❑ **Who** — List important nouns: author, recipients, persons, or things.

3❑ **What** — is the subject, theme, or topic? Or the circumstances and events? Briefly state the main facts or ideas in your own words.

4❑ **When** — Note references to **times** (past, present, future) or **seasons**.

5❑ **Where** — are the locations/events of this chapter taking place?

6❑ Why — Write down anything that reveals an **objective** [thing aimed at or sought] **or purpose** [intention, object to be reached or accomplished, reason something is done]?

____

____

____

____

7❑ How — Record the manner, means, way, degree, or extent to which the **doctrine** [whatever is taught] or **teaching** [instruction to educate and impart knowledge] is communicated, illustrated, learned, or received.

____

____

____

____

8❑ List the six most essential or repeated words or phrases.

1 ______________ 4 ______________

2 ______________ 5 ______________

3 ______________ 6 ______________

9❑ Share something you found interesting, odd, or hard to understand.

____

____

____

1❑ Take *2 to 3 minutes* to read all 10 verses of Jonah **Chapter 2**.

2❑ **Who** — List important nouns: author, recipients, persons, or things.

3❑ **What** — is the subject, theme, or topic? Or the circumstances and events? Briefly state the main facts or ideas in your own words.

4❑ **When** — Note references to **times** (past, present, future) or **seasons**.

5❑ **Where** — are the locations/events of this chapter taking place?

6❑ **Why** – Write down anything that reveals an **objective** [thing aimed at or sought] **or purpose** [intention, object to be reached or accomplished, reason something is done]?

7❑ **How** – Record the manner, means, way, degree, or extent to which the **doctrine** [whatever is taught] or **teaching** [instruction to educate and impart knowledge] is communicated, illustrated, learned, or received.

8❑ List the six most essential or repeated words or phrases.

1 ______________ 4 ______________

2 ______________ 5 ______________

3 ______________ 6 ______________

9❑ Share something you found interesting, odd, or hard to understand.

Observe—Chapter 3

1❏ Take *2 to 3 minutes* to read all 10 verses of Jonah **Chapter 3**.

2❏ **Who** — List important nouns: author, recipients, persons, or things.

3❏ **What** — is the subject, theme, or topic? Or the circumstances and events? Briefly state the main facts or ideas in your own words.

4❏ **When** — Note references to **times** (past, present, future) or **seasons**.

5❏ **Where** — are the locations/events of this chapter taking place?

6❑ **Why** — Write down anything that reveals an **objective** [thing aimed at or sought] **or purpose** [intention, object to be reached or accomplished, reason something is done]?

7❑ **How** — Record the manner, means, way, degree, or extent to which the **doctrine** [whatever is taught] or **teaching** [instruction to educate and impart knowledge] is communicated, illustrated, learned, or received.

8❑ List the six most essential or repeated words or phrases.

1 ______ 4 ______

2 ______ 5 ______

3 ______ 6 ______

9❑ Share something you found interesting, odd, or hard to understand.

1❑ Take *2 to 3 minutes* to read all 11 verses of Jonah **Chapter 4**.

2❑ **Who** — List important nouns: author, recipients, persons, or things.

3❑ **What** — is the subject, theme, or topic? Or the circumstances and events? Briefly state the main facts or ideas in your own words.

4❑ **When** — Note references to **times** (past, present, future) or **seasons**.

5❑ **Where** — are the locations/events of this chapter taking place?

6❑ **Why** — Write down anything that reveals an **objective** [thing aimed at or sought] **or purpose** [intention, object to be reached or accomplished, reason something is done]?

____

____

____

____

7❑ **How** — Record the manner, means, way, degree, or extent to which the **doctrine** [whatever is taught] **or teaching** [instruction to educate and impart knowledge] is communicated, illustrated, learned, or received.

____

____

____

____

8❑ List the six most essential or repeated words or phrases.

1 ____________________ 4 ____________________

2 ____________________ 5 ____________________

3 ____________________ 6 ____________________

9❑ Share something you found interesting, odd, or hard to understand.

____

____

____

Creative Challenge

Throughout this study, you will find stress-less coloring backgrounds and empty or lined frame boxes to inspire personal creativity.

Coloring is proven **therapeutic** [having beneficial effects on the body or mind]. Coloring enthusiasts find that decisions, details, patterns, and repetition reduce anxiety and stress.

By calming your thoughts as you focus on creativity, the cares of the day are less likely to consume your attention. Express what impresses upon your heart/mind using your God-given talents.

Mixing it up between reading, meditating on God's word, study, and creative/artistic expression will keep you Busy in the Bible™.

Try Bible Verse Art

1) Pick a verse from the chapter.

2) Sketch in the words you want to bring attention to first, leaving space to add the rest of the verse above, below, or around it. Include the Bible book, chapter, and verse number.

3) Use your imagination to make the verse visually expressive.

Note: If you enjoy arts and crafts but don't feel exceptionally gifted in drawing, trace something from an inspirational piece of art you admire. Place the art you want to copy under a blank piece of paper or under the frame to the left. Hold both pages together up to a window to make it easier to see lines to trace over.

Or, use the following ideas to inspire, but not limit, your thinking.

- ❍ **Children's stories**
- ❍ **Clothing Design**
- ❍ **Coloring/Tracing**
- ❍ **Creative writing**
- ❍ **Drama/Skit writing**
- ❍ **Drawing/Illustration**
- ❍ **Games**
- ❍ **Music composition/Song lyrics**
- ❍ **Poetry/Poems**
- ❍ **Puzzles/Riddles/Rhymes**
- ❍ **Quiz Creation**
- ❍ **Trivia-type Questions**

Date: ___________

Amplified Bible Study—

The word **amplified** means [to make or cause to be larger, more extended, or more intense; to communicate thoughts with many words, expand by adding particulars, illustrations, etc.; to make much of].

This study defines hundreds of words you may or may not know. This is done to provide clear communication on any subject covered and avoid misunderstanding questions presented. While reading you will find words you might not know well in bold, followed by their **definition** [what a word is understood to express] in brackets. If you find the educational assistance unnecessary, ignore the bracketed text.

Bible scholars and translators are challenged with communicating the precise intent and meaning of Hebrew and Greek words using singular words in English. Amplification of biblical words in this study is not equivalent to a scholarly translation of God's word.

Note: Question numbers reset to 1 for each verse of focus.

Resources—

Words are defined using a combination of the following resources:

An American Dictionary of the English Language (1828) Noah Webster Jr. Mr. Webster established a system of rules to govern spelling, grammar, and reading, using the Bible as the foundation for his definitions. He considered education without the Bible "useless."

Gesenius' Hebrew and Chaldee Lexicon Wilhelm Gesenius (1786–1842) Professor and Bible scholar. Gesenius was a Professor and Bible scholar. Gesenius was a German-born master of Hebrew. Upon his passing, Samuel P. Tregelles edited and translated his documents into English.

Strong's Exhaustive Concordance of the Bible (1890) with dictionaries. This concordance indexes every word in the King

James Version (KJV) and assigns a "Strong's number" to the root words. It provides transliteration, which means it converts a word from a different language into letters you can understand (Hebrew to English). It also provides the etymology showing how a simple root word developed into the word used at the time of translation. It should not be considered sufficient for sound hermeneutics (the principle of interpreting and expounding the Scriptures) but can be a starting point.

If possible, join with others—

The challenge of independent study in a workbook like this is that the writer, communicating and teaching on paper, cannot gauge if the learner has sensible answers and sound-minded understanding.

If possible, please join a Bible study group, start a small group, or interact with your religious/spiritual leader to discuss answers and enjoy **fellowship** [have companionship; society; mutual association with others on equal and friendly terms; communion].

> *Proverbs 11:14* **Where no counsel is, the people fall: but in the multitude of counselors there is safety.**

Pause & Persevere—

Throughout this study, we'll ◁ **pause** [temporary rest; intermission; ceasing or intermission of action] from the text of Jonah to increase your knowledge and understanding of **correlated** [to compare things and bring them into a relation having corresponding characteristics] information. Returning, you'll ▷ **persevere** [to persist in any enterprise undertaken; to pursue steadily any design or course commenced; not to give over or abandon what is undertaken].

Let's begin a detailed verse-by-verse journey through Jonah Chapter 1.

1❑ From the *birth* of Jesus Christ, our calendar year dates *forward*. The abbreviation A.D. comes from the Latin phrase ***a**nno **d**omini,* which means "in the year of our Lord." It is shown like this: A.D. 1

................................Record today's date: _ _ /_ _ /_ _ _ _.
month day year

How many years have passed since Jesus was born? _ _ _ _.
year (same as above)

This system of dating began a few centuries after Christ's birth. The birth of Jesus Christ **is** the pivotal point in world history. Modern scholars believe the dating may be off by a few years. Yet, the entire world uses this dating and year designation no matter their belief, i.e., Christian, Jewish, Muslim, Hindu, Buddhist, Atheist, Agnostic, etc.

Before Jesus' birth, the calendar dates *backward*. The year before His birth is noted as 1 B.C. (or 1 BC), which means **B**efore **C**hrist. The Book of Jonah is believed to have occurred during the Eighth Century (between 799—700 BC). So, over 700 years before Christ's birth.

The Biblical books near the time of Jonah are:

	Occurred	*Written*
Jonah	786—760 BC	775 BC
Amos	767—753 BC	750 BC
Micah	750—686 BC	735—710 BC
Hosea	790—686 BC	715 BC
Isaiah	739—681 BC	700—681 BC

Bible scholars disagree on the exact dating of both the writing and occurrences.

Which book was written farthest from today? _ _ _ _ _

List the books in order of the *beginning* of occurrences:

_ _ _ _ _ .... 790—686 BC
_ _ _ _ _ .... 786—760 BC
_ _ _ _ .... 767—753 BC
_ _ _ _ _ .... 750—686 BC
_ _ _ _ _ _ ... 739-681 BC

2❑ The Book of Amos records events when Uzziah was king of Judah and Jeroboam II was king of Israel. By inspiration of God, Amos, a prophet, warned of judgment ahead for those exploiting the poor and disadvantaged. At that time, spiritual corruption, disregard for human rights, and decaying morality were rampant. The corrupt were not grieved over their sin. Yet, like today, God's warnings included _ _ _ _ * for those who seek Him:

Amos 5:6 (✍750 BC) **Seek the LORD, and you shall live.**

* _ _ _ _ **is defined as** [a desire of some good, accompanied with at least a slight expectation of obtaining it, or a belief that it is obtainable].

▲ *Note: It is common for believers to interchange the words God and LORD (Lord). They are two different words with distinct differences, yet the Bible teaches they refer to the same One God.*

God 'ĕlôhîm *el-o-**heem*** [H430 ɴ *the Supreme God; the God of Abraham; God of gods; true God; God of all flesh] as found in Genesis 1:1 and Jonah 1:5.*

LORD Yehôvâh *yeh-ho-**vaw*** [H3068 ɴ *the existing One, self-Existent Eternal], as found in Genesis 2:4, Amos 5:6, and Jonah 1:9.*

3❑ Hosea was a prophet, evangelist, and contemporary of Amos. The Book of Hosea reveals Hosea's pleadings to reach the people of the northern kingdom before they became captives of the evil Assyrians. The priests and prophets were not ministering the word of God. Consequently, the people lacked knowledge. Hosea's biography is like no other. God told him to marry a wife of whoredoms to graphically illustrate unfaithfulness and its effects. Hosea's message? Salvation, grace, pardon, mercy, and restoration await those who respond to the conviction of sin with genuine **repentance** [change of mind]. Despite looming chastisement, God's message to Israel and their future hope* is foretold:

Hosea 2:23 (✍715 BC) **And I will sow her** [scatter Israel's† seed] **to Me in the earth; and I will have mercy upon her that had not obtained mercy; and I will say to them which were not My People, you are My people; and they shall say, You are my God.** † *Added for clarity*

Jonah 1:1 Now the word of the Lord came to Jonah the son of Amittai, saying,

1❏ It is important to learn about the book's main person, Jonah (also spelled Jonas), who is nearly pronounced Yoh-**naw**. The Hebrew name and meaning are the same for *Dove*. Dove is a term of endearment used to describe something or someone gentle, feeble, or weak. A dove is sometimes used to symbolize hope, love, peace, or tranquility.

If you have ever encountered a dove, share what you know of their **behavior** [conduct; manners], **personality** [distinct characteristics], or **temperament** [inborn traits; habits; reactions]:

2❏ ***IF*** Jonah's name was given by the inspiration of God and **indicative** [showing; giving intimation or knowledge of something not visible or obvious] of his tendencies, what *might* his personality have been like?

3❏ Look back at your chapter observations (pages ***28—29***). Does the Book of Jonah reveal its author .... ❍Yes ❍No ❍?

4❏ Jonah's father's name is _ _ _ _ _ _ _ [my truth].

5❑ Read the following cross reference or look it up in your Bible to have a better understanding of its **context** [surrounding verses]:

2 Kings 14:25 (✍561–538 BC) **He** *(Jeroboam II†)* **restored the coast of Israel from the entering of Hamath to the sea of the plain, according to the word of the LORD God of Israel, which he spoke by the hand of his servant Jonah, the son of Amittai, the prophet, which was of Gathhepher.** *†Added for clarity*

Although Jeroboam II did evil in the sight of the LORD, God used him to do some good since the affliction of Israel was very bitter.

Whom did God use to speak to Jeroboam II? _ _ _ _ _

Was Jonah a servant of God? .... ❍Yes ❍No ❍?

Was Jonah a prophet of God?.. ❍Yes ❍No ❍?

6❑ In the time of Joshua, **lots** [sticks, stones, dice] were cast to divide the land among the children of Israel. The third lot chose the children of Zebulun's land, where Jonah's hometown, Gath Hepher, was.

Joshua 19:13a (✍1405–1385 BC) **And from there passes on along on the east to Gath Hepher...**

What famous town was Gath Hepher near? _ _ _ _ _ _ _ _

▲ *Note: You might find Gath Hepher spelled Gittah-hepher based on your Bible's translation.*

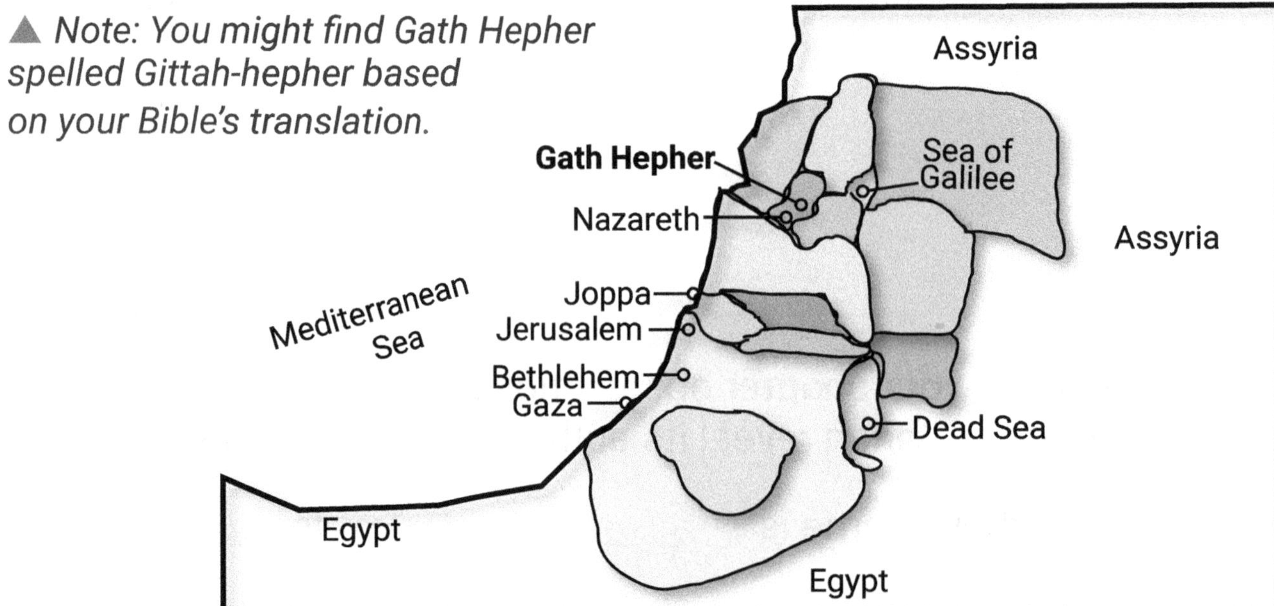

7❑ Now that we have a background of Jonah's heritage, let's return to the details in Jonah 1:1. Who spoke to Jonah? ________________

8❑ In this study, you will find a combination of the following sources *inserted after a word* to help you know the closest definition for words used in the Bible:

✓1890 Strong's Concordance Dictionary ✓1828 Webster's Dictionary
✓Brown-Driver-Briggs Lexicon ✓Gesenius' Hebrew-Chaldee Lexicon

Here is an example of every Hebrew word/phrase defined in verse 1:

1:1 **Now the word** [H169 *n* word, speech, discourse; saying, utterance; promise; precept; edict; counsel, proposed plan; report; thing, thing done] **of the Lord** Yehôvâh *yeh-ho-**vaw*** [YHWH H3068 *n* the existing One, self-Existent Eternal] **came** [H1961 v to be, become; come to pass; exist; happen; occur; come about, come to pass; come into being; to arise, appear **to** [H413 *prep* motion towards] **Jonah** *yoh-**naw*** [H3124 *n* DOVE; a gentle term of endearment; weak, gentle, feeble] **the son** [H1121 *n* builder of the family name] **of Amittai,** *am-it-**tie*** [H573 *n* MY TRUTH; veracious: habitually disposed to speak truth] **saying,** [H559 v to answer, bear forth, bring to light, declare; to say in the heart (to think); to promise; command]

Key to the definition box:

of the Lord *yeh-ho-**vaw*** [YHWH H3068 *n* the existing One, self-Existent Eternal]

Word/phrase — pronunciation — Strong's # — Grammar — Dictionary/Lexicon Definitions

The words in **bold** are from the *King James Today* Bible translation. The meaning of a name is shown in small all caps, *e.g.*, Jonah's name means DOVE.

▲ *Note:*

i.e.=*An abbreviation of the Latin phrase id est, meaning "that is." It is used to clarify or reword.*

e.g.=*An abbreviation of the Latin phrase exempli gratia, meaning "for example." You can remember it as an "example given." It is used to illustrate what has been stated.*

9❑ Write what "**the word** of the Lord" means (look it up with your own resources or refer to the definition box (*page* ***45***, question 2).

____

____

____

____

10❑ How would you explain the definition of "**the Lord**" *yeh-ho-***vaw**:

____

____

____

____

11❑ The word of the Lord came to Jonah. But how? Review the definition of **came**, then take a moment to *guess possible ways* the Lord might have "spoken" to Jonah.

1 ______________ 2 ______________

3 ______________ 4 ______________

5 ______________ 6 ______________

7 ______________ 8 ______________

12❑ Have you ever read or heard something from the Bible that gave you a sense of God's **leading** [showing the way; directing or guiding]? .... ❍Yes ❍No ❍?

13❑ Did Jonah hear the Lord audibly (out loud)?......... ❍Yes ❍No ❍?

14❑ Where was Jonah when 1:1 occurred? ______________

PAUSE Jonah 1:1

A❏ **1** God communicates **through hearing/reading/seeing/studying His word**, the Holy Bible.

2 Timothy 3:16–17 (✍AD 66–67) *16* **All scripture is given by inspiration of God, and is profitable for doctrine, for reproof, for correction, for instruction in righteousness:** *17* **That the man of God may be perfect, thoroughly furnished to all good works.**

If you believe God has used His word to "speak" to you, share what happened along with the Bible book name, chapter, and verse number, **a**lso **k**nown **a**s *(aka)* ***the scripture address, citation, reference, or source***. For example, Genesis 1:1.
Genesis (the book), 1 (the chapter): 1 (the verse number).

☆ It would be nice to talk with someone about this subject.

B❑ The following is a list of books of the Bible and the approximate date each was written. On the left are the books written up to the Book of Jonah, and on the right are those written after.

Book: Approximate date written

▲ *Note: Bible scholars disagree on the exact dating of biblical books.*

Job: Date unknown *(considered the oldest book ever written)*

Genesis: 1445—1405 BC
Exodus: 1445—1405 BC
Leviticus: 1445—1405 BC
Numbers: 1445—1405 BC
Deuteronomy: 1445—1405 BC
Psalms: 1410—450 BC
Joshua: 1405—1385 BC
Judges: 1043 BC
Ruth: 1030—1010
Song of Songs: 971—965 BC
Proverbs: 971—686 BC
Ecclesiastes: 940—931 BC
1 Samuel: 931—722 BC
2 Samuel: 931—722 BC
Obadiah: 850—840 BC
Joel: 835—796 BC
<u>Jonah</u>: 775 BC

Amos: 750
Hosea: 750—710 BC
Micah: 735—710 BC
Isaiah: 700—681 BC
Nahum: 650 BC
Zephaniah: 635—625 BC
Habakkuk: 615—605 BC
Ezekiel: 590—570 BC
Lamentations: 586 BC
Jeremiah: 586—570
1 Kings: 561—538 BC
2 Kings: 561—538 BC
Daniel: 536—530 BC
Haggai: 520 BC
Zechariah: 480—470 BC
Ezra: 457—444 BC
1 Chronicles: 450—430
2 Chronicles: 450—430 BC
Esther: 450—331 BC
Malachi: 433—424 BC
Nehemiah: 424—400 BC

Is it reasonable to believe Jonah was familiar with God's word (either by hearing, reading, seeing, studying, or proclaiming it)? .... ❍Yes ❍No ❍?

Has God's word ever come into your mind/thoughts .. ❍Yes ❍No ❍?

C❑ **2** God communicates **during prayer and Biblical meditation***. I have sensed God guiding me *to or away from* something while in prayer.. ❍Agree ❍Disagree ❍?

Share your experience:

☆ It would be nice to talk with someone about this subject.

*There are five different definitions of **meditation** and three different definitions of **meditate** used in the Old Testament.

Let's begin with understanding "meditation."

I: Meditation H1900 hāgût *haw-**gooth*** *n* [thought (that which the mind thinks; idea; conception; something framed by the imagination; reflection; opinion; judgment; serious consideration; care; concern; inward reasoning), meditation (close or continued thought; the turning or revolving of a subject in the mind; serious contemplation), musing (meditation in silence)]

Psalm 49:3 (✍799–700 BC) **My mouth shall speak of wisdom; and the** meditation **of my heart shall be of understanding.**

The Hebrew word hāgût is described in English using the following word:

1 ______________________________

II: Meditation, *Musing* H1901 hâgîyg *haw-**gheeg*** n [a murmur to grumble; to complain; to utter complaints in a low, half articulated voice; to utter sullen discontent); complaint (expression of grief, regret, pain, sickness, censure, or resentment; lamentation; murmuring; a finding fault); whisper (to utter in a low hissing voice) or musing (contemplation, continued attention of the mind to a particular subject, in silence), stemming from the root word for heat (redness of the face, flush; inflammation or excitement; agitation of mind), fervor (warm or animated zeal and earnestness of mind]

Psalm 5:1 (✍1000–900 BC) **Give ear to my words, O LORD, consider my** meditation**.**

Psalm 39:3 (✍1000–900 BC) **My heart was hot within me, while I was** musing **the fire burned: then spoke I with my tongue,**

The Hebrew word hâgîyg is described in English using the following two words:

1 ______________________________ 2______________________________

III: Meditation, *Higgaion, Solemn Sound, Device* H1902 higāyôn *hig-gaw-**yohn*** n [a murmuring sound, i.e., a musical note to indicate solemnity (serious religious reverence to impress awe), resounding (echoing) music, meditation or contemplation in silence, sounding music upon the lyre; the sound of a harp when struck. ***Used in a bad sense:*** a machination (planning or contriving a scheme for executing some purpose, particularly an evil purpose); a device (that which is formed by design or invented; scheme; artificial contrivance; stratagem; project employed for bad purposes.), a plot (any scheme, stratagem or plan of a complicated nature, or consisting of many parts, adapted to the accomplishment of some purpose, usually a mischievous one)]

Psalm 9:16 (✍1000–900 BC) **The LORD is known by the judgment which he executes: the wicked is snared in the work of his own hands.** Higgaion. **Selah.**

Psalm 19:14 (✍1000–900 BC) **Let the words of my mouth, and the** meditation **of my heart, be acceptable in thy sight, O LORD, my strength, and my redeemer.**

Psalm 92:3 (✍539–500 BC) **Upon an instrument of ten strings, and upon the psaltery; upon the harp with a** solemn sound**.**

Lamentations 3:63 (✍586 BC) **The lips of those that rose up against me, and their** device **against me all the day.**

The Hebrew word higāyôn is described in English using the following words or phrases:

1 ______________________ 2 ______________________

3 ______________________ 4 ______________________

IV: Meditation, *Complaint, Talking, Communication, Prayer, Babbling* H7879 śîah ***see**-akh*n [the musings (meditation in silence) of man; a contemplation; by implication, an utterance, babbling, communication, complaint, meditation, prayer, talk]

1 Samuel 1:16 (✍931–722 BC) **Count not your handmaid for a daughter of Belial: for out of the abundance of my** complaint **and grief have I spoken hitherto.**

1 Kings 18:27 (✍561–538 BC) **And it came to pass at noon, that Elijah mocked them, and said, Cry aloud: for he is a god; either he is** talking**, or he is pursuing, or he is in a journey, or peradventure he sleeps, and must be awaked.**

2 Kings 9:11 (✍561–538 BC) **Then Jehu came forth to the servants of his lord: and one said to him, Is all well? wherefore came this mad fellow to you? And he said to them, You know the man, and his** communication**.**

- ❍ *Job 7:13* (✍1450–1350 BC) complaint
- ❍ *Job 9:27*(✍1450–1350 BC) complaint
- ❍ *Job 10:1* ((✍1450–1350 BC) complaint
- ❍ *Job 21:4* (✍1450–1350 BC) complaint
- ❍ *Job 23:2* (✍1450–1350 BC) complaint
- ❍ *Psalm 55:2* (✍1000–900 BC) complaint

Psalm 64:1 (✍1000–900 BC) **[To the chief Musician, A Psalm of David.] Hear my voice, O God, in my** prayer**: preserve my life from fear of the enemy.**

- ❍ *Psalm 102:1* (✍586–539 BC) complaint

Psalm 104:34 (✍899–800 BC) **My** meditation **of him shall be sweet: I will be glad in the LORD.**

- ❍ *Psalm 142:2* (✍1000–900 BC)complaint

Proverbs 23:29 (✍971–686 BC) **Who has woe? who has sorrow? who has contentions? who has** babbling**? who has wounds without cause? who has redness of eyes?**

The Hebrew word śîah is described in English using the following unique words:

1 ______________________	4 ______________________
2 ______________________	5 ______________________
3 ______________________	6 ______________________

V: Meditation H7881 śîhâ *see-**khaw*** n [reflection (the operation of the mind by which it turns its views back upon itself and its operations; the review or consideration of past thoughts, opinions or decisions of the mind, or of past events; the expression of thought; attentive consideration); devotion (the state of being dedicated, consecrated, or solemnly set apart for a particular purpose; solemn attention to the Supreme Being in worship; a yielding of the heart and affections to God, with reverence, faith, and piety, in religious duties, particularly in prayer and meditation; devoutness; prayer to the Supreme Being); prayer; meditation especially pious (Godly; reverencing and honoring the Supreme Being in heart and in the practice of the duties He has enjoined; having due veneration and affection for the character of God, and habitually obeying his commands; religious; devoted to the service of God), relating to divine (pertaining to the true God) things]

Job 15:4 **Yea, you cast off fear, and restrain** prayer **before God.**

Psalm 119:97 (✍499–400 BC) **O how love I your law! it is my** meditation **all the day.**

○ *Psalm 119:99* (✍499–400 BC) meditation**.**

The Hebrew word śîhâ is described in English using the following two words:

1 ______________________________ 2______________________________

As you have learned, multiple English words are used to describe the different Hebrew words that define meditation.

As previously mentioned, there are three different definitions of **meditate** used in the Old Testament as follows:

i: Meditate H7742 śûah *shoo-**ahkh*** v [to muse (ponder, think closely, study in silence; to be absent in mind; to be so occupied in study or contemplation, as not to observe passing scenes or things present) pensively (With thoughtfulness; with gloomy seriousness or some degree of melancholy).

Genesis 24:63 (✍1450–1410 BC) **And Isaac went out to** meditate **in the field at the eventide: and he lifted up his eyes, and saw, and, behold, the camels were coming.**

ii: Meditate H7878 śîah *she-**ahkh*** v [to muse (ponder, think closely, study in silence; to be absent in mind; to be so occupied in study or contemplation, as not to observe passing scenes or things present) pensively (With thoughtfulness; with gloomy seriousness or some degree of melancholy).

Psalm 119:15 (✍499–400 BC) **I will** meditate **in your precepts, and have respect to your ways.**

- ❍ *Psalm 119:23* (✍499–400 BC) meditate
- ❍ *Psalm 119:48* (✍499–400 BC) meditate
- ❍ *Psalm 119:78* (✍499–400 BC) meditate
- ❍ *Psalm 119:14* (✍499–400 BC) meditate

iii: Meditate H1897 hāgâ *haw-**ghaw*** v [to murmur (in pleasure or anger); by implication, to ponder; imagine, meditate, mourn, mutter, mourn sore, speak, study, talk, utter; to growl like a lion over its prey, to roar; of low thunder; of the sound of a harp when struck; of the cooing of doves; of the groaning and sighing of men; poetically to speak, utter sound, sing, celebrate; to meditate or speak with oneself, murmuring and in a low voice as is often done by those who are musing; also to remember anything. In a bad sense, to plot, to plan, to devise; to contemplate; to murmur or utter an inarticulate sound such as a growl, groan, moan, sigh]

- ❍ *Psalm 1:2* (✍499–400 BC)
- ❍ *Psalm 63:6* (✍1000–900 BC)
- ❍ *Psalm 77:12* (✍799–700 BC)
- ❍ *Psalm 143:5* (✍1000–900 BC)
- ❍ *Isaiah 33:18* (✍799–700 BC)

Joshua 1:8 (✍1000–900 BC) **This book of the law shall not depart out of your mouth; but you shall** meditate **therein day and night, that you may observe to do according to all that is written therein: for then you shall make your way prosperous, and then you shall have good success.**

What are the three things Joshua is commanded by God:

1 ______________________________

2 ______________________________

3 ______________________________

What are the two benefits given for obedience to God's commands:

1 ______________

2 ______________

D❑ Is it likely a prophet of God, such as Jonah, understood God's command in Joshua 1:8 should be his own habit .. ❍True ❍False ❍?

E❑ Biblical meditation is a regular habit of mine .... ❍True ❍False ❍?

Why, why not, or what would you like to change?

____

____

____

____

____

____

____

Date: ____________

F❑ **3** God communicates **through the Holy Spirit**, *aka*: Holy Ghost, holy ghost, holy Spirit, holy spirit, Spirit, spirit. There are many other words referring to the Holy Spirit, and much more to learn, which would be an entirely different Bible study. Here are a few verses that will help you know how to be in God's will, recognize His leading, and follow Him as a Believer.

> *John 14:26* (✍AD 80–90) **But the Comforter, which is the Holy Ghost, whom the Father will send in my name, he shall teach you all things, and bring all things to your remembrance, whatsoever I have said to you.**

What is another name for the Holy Ghost according to John 14:26:

1 ____________________________

There are many functions of the Holy Ghost. What are two of them:

1 ____________________________

2 ____________________________

G❑ Here are some attributes of the Holy Spirit:

I) The Holy Spirit distributes spiritual gifts (read *1 Corinthians 12*).

II) The Holy Spirit comforts us:

> *John 14:16* (✍AD 80–90) **And I will pray the Father, and he shall give you another <u>Comforter</u>, that he may abide with you for ever;**

III) The Holy Spirit reveals the things of God:

> *2 Corinthians 2:9–11* (✍AD 55–56) *9* **But as it is written, Eye has not seen, nor ear heard, neither have entered into the heart of man, the things which God hath prepared for them that love him.**
> *10* **But God has revealed them to us by <u>his Spirit</u>: for the Spirit searches all things, yea, the deep things of God.** *11* **For what**

man knows the things of a man, save the spirit of man which is in him? even so the things of God knows no man, but the Spirit of God.

IV)The Holy Spirit reproves of sin, righteousness, and judgment:

John 16:7–11 (✍AD 80–90) *7* **Nevertheless I** *[Jesus†]* **tell you the truth; It is expedient for you that I go away: for if I go not away, the Comforter will not come to you; but if I depart, I will send him to you.** *8* **And when he is come, he will reprove the world of sin, and of righteousness, and of judgment:** *9* **Of sin, because they believe not on me;** *10* **Of righteousness, because I go to my Father, and you see me no more;** *11* **Of judgment, because the prince of this world is judged.** *†Added for clarity*

V) The Holy Spirit guides you into all truth, and shows things to come:

John 16:12–14 (✍AD 80–90) *12* **I have yet many things to say to you, but you cannot bear them now. 13 Howbeit when he, the Spirit of truth, is come, he will guide you into all truth: for he shall not speak of himself; but whatsoever he shall hear, that shall he speak: and he will show you things to come.** *14* **He shall glorify me: for he shall receive of mine, and shall show it to you.**

VI) The Holy Spirit helps our feebleness of mind, body, and soul. He searches our heart and intercedes on our behalf.

Romans 8:26–27 (✍AD 56) *26* **Likewise the Spirit also helps our infirmities: for we know not what we should pray for as we ought: but the Spirit itself makes intercession for us with groanings which cannot be uttered.** *27* **And he that searches the hearts knows what is the mind of the Spirit, because he makes intercession for the saints according to the will of God.**

H❑ If something conflicts with or is contrary to God's word...

...is it the guidance of God? ....❍Correct ❍Incorrect ❍?

...is it the Holy Spirit's leading? ....❍Correct ❍Incorrect ❍?

I❑ If something conflicts with or is contrary to God's word...

...I must proceed with caution........................... ❍True ❍False ❍?

...I should stop or pause my decision .... ❍True ❍False ❍?

...I will seek a multitude of wise counselors...... ❍True ❍False ❍?

...Study biblical text for accurate understanding.. ❍True ❍False ❍?

J❑ Share if you have an experience you believe was the Holy Spirit "speaking" to you or of a time you did not heed His guidance:

☆ It would be nice to talk with someone about this subject.

K❑ Starting on page ***47***, notice the bold numbers like this: **123**. Summarize the principal ways Believers are guided by God.

1 ____________________ ❑

2 ____________________ ❑

3 ____________________ ❑

Mark the box to the right if you have experienced God in this way.

L❑ Learning the Bible consists of believing things literally (real, as they are) and questioning things you do or do not understand. It takes an investigative mindset to go beyond reading into inquiring. There isn't enough written in the Bible to answer every question a person can think of or encounter. There is no easy verse to go to for every decision you must make, but plenty to guide us and teach us about God's character and heart. You must figure out how to apply scripture accurately to your circumstances. And that means you need to spend plenty of time in God's word, prayer, and practical application of what you learn. You will get some things right and some things wrong. We all experience success and failure.

Is it spiritually healthy to ask questions about the Bible to be fully convinced of what you believe? .... ❍Agree ❍Disagree ❍?

M❑ It might seem too basic to review this, but to study the Bible, you have to **think** v [to have the mind occupied on some subject; to have or revolve ideas in the mind; to judge; to conclude; to hold as a settled opinion; to imagine; to suppose; to believe, esteem; to muse in deep thought; contemplation, ponder, wonder, study in silence].

Biblical meditation involves close or continued *thinking* of an idea or subject in the mind. Yet it doesn't mean your thinking is biblically correct. That's why cross-referencing, reading, studying, and accurately applying the Bible is essential.

Honestly, how often do you *read to understand* the Bible, meaning slow enough to ponder/meditate on its teaching? Use this space to write a brief prayer on this topic:

____

____

____

Date: __________

N❑ The apostle Paul warned of combining philosophy with **vain** [empty; devoid of truth] **deceit:**

> *Colossians 2:8* (✍AD 60–62) **Beware lest any man spoil you through philosophy and vain deceit, after the tradition of men, after the rudiments of the world, and not after Christ.**

The Greek word for **philosophy** is *philosophia*: **philo** meaning [love], plus **sophia** meaning [wisdom]; [the love of wisdom]. That alone seems to line up with the Bible, but Paul's warning was to beware of certain Jewish Christians caught up in **sophistry** [fallacious/deceptive reasoning], consumed with **speculative** [theoretical; not verified by fact, experiment, or practice] inquiry of angels, Mosaic law, and Jewish traditions. Mankind tends to believe everything in the world can be understood or explained.

Why do students of the Bible need to be cautious of things that cannot be verified in God's word:

____

____

____

Can everything in the world be explained..................... ❍Yes ❍No ❍?
Can you explain everything in the world .... ❍Yes ❍No ❍?
Can everything in the world be understood................. ❍Yes ❍No ❍?
Can you understand everything in the world .... ❍Yes ❍No ❍?
Can students of the Bible be misled............................ ❍Yes ❍No ❍?
Can you be deceived, misled, or in error .... ❍Yes ❍No ❍?
Can you misinterpret scripture from the bias of mind. ❍Yes ❍No ❍?
.... from ignorance .... ❍Yes ❍No ❍?
.... from inattention.......... ❍Yes ❍No ❍?
.... from poor judgment ... ❍Yes ❍No ❍?

O❑ What is the definition of philosophy? **Philosophy** *fuh-**laa**-suh-fee* *n* [a general term denoting an explanation of the reasons of things or an investigation of the causes of all phenomena both of mind and of matter. When applied to any particular department of knowledge, it denotes the collection of general laws or principles under which all the subordinate phenomena or facts relating to that subject are comprehended. Thus, that branch of philosophy which treats (handles in a particular manner of writing or speaking) of God, etc., is called theology; that which treats of nature is called physics or natural philosophy; that which treats of man is called logic and ethics, or moral philosophy; that which treats of the mind is called intellectual or mental philosophy or metaphysics].

All philosophy is: ❍wrong ❍worldly................ ❍Agree ❍Disagree ❍?

Which philosophical knowledge investigates the existence, facts, laws, principles, reasons, truth, or understanding of God? _ _ _ _ _ _ _ _

P❑ Keep the following definitions in mind as you are challenged in this study to **determine** [decide, conclude] why you believe as you do:

Fact *n* [any thing done, or that comes to pass; an act or deed; an effect produced or achieved; an event; reality (actual being or existence of anything); truth]

All determinations or decisions are based on facts..❍True ❍False ❍?

Feeling *n* [The sense of touch by which you perceive external objects that come in contact with your body; the effect of emotions]

Might some decisions be based on feelings .... ❍Yes ❍No ❍?

Guess *n/v* [*aka* conjecture; an opinion formed without certain principles, means of knowledge, experience, or logic, or from reasons that render a thing probable or possible on very slight or no evidence; opinion at random]

Might some determinations be based on guessing .... ❍Yes ❍No ❍?

If you can only guess, should you seek wise counsel?...... ❍Y ❍N ❍?

Hypothesis *hi-pah-thuh-sis* *n* [an assumption used as a basis for reasoning or as a starting point to investigate for evidence of truth to draw a conclusion]

Will some of your determinations be a hypothesis ..... ❍Yes ❍No ❍?

Theory *n* [that which is offered for acceptance, adoption, or consideration drawn from another which is admitted or supposed to be true; general principles which have been established on independent evidence]

Will some of your determinations be theory .... ❍Yes ❍No ❍?

Investigation *n* [to inquire and examine into with care and accuracy; to find out through careful, systematic inquiry into a subject by arguments or discussion of the facts and circumstances that may make clear, explain, or illustrate truth]

Does Bible study require investigation .... ❍Yes ❍No ❍?

Theology *thee-**ah**-luh-jee* *n* [the science (knowledge, understanding of truth and facts) which teaches the attributes, character, existence, nature, providence, and power of God, His laws and government, the doctrines we are to believe, and the duties we are to practice. Theology consists of two branches: natural (the knowledge we have of God from His works, by the light of nature and reason) and revealed (the disclosure or communication of truth, before unknown or concealed, to men by God or by His authorized agents, the prophets and apostles)]

Attribute *n* [that which is considered as belonging to, or inherent in; a quality determining something to be after a certain manner]

Characteristic *n* [that which distinguishes a person or thing from another]

Doctrine *n* [In a general sense, whatever is taught as true by an instructor or master]

Nature *n* [the agent, creator, author, producer of things, or the powers that produce them; a word that comprehends all the works of God]

Providence *n* [the care and superintendence which God exercises over his creatures; timely care; foresight accompanied with the procurement of what is necessary for future use, or with suitable preparation]

PERSEVERE Jonah 1:1

15❑ As a son, Jonah has a responsibility within his family. What is the responsibility of a son? (review the definition on page ***45***)

____

16❑ Could a daughter have the same responsibility? . ❍Yes ❍No ❍?

17❑ ***IF*** Jonah's father's name was given by the inspiration of God and **indicative** [giving intimation or knowledge of something not visible or obvious] of his **personality** *n* [cognitive (mentally acquiring knowledge and understanding through personal experience, the senses, and thoughts), and emotional patterns of behavior] what might Amittai be known for:

____

____

18❑ Does Jonah 1:1 give any indication **the word** of the Lord came to Jonah while he was...

...*hearing* Biblical text, scripture, the word of God ...... ❍Yes ❍No ❍?
...*reading* Biblical text, scripture, the word of God ...... ❍Yes ❍No ❍?
...*seeing* Biblical text, scripture, the word of God........ ❍Yes ❍No ❍?
...*studying* Biblical text, scripture, the word of God..... ❍Yes ❍No ❍?
...while he was *praying* .... ❍Yes ❍No ❍?
...when he was *meditating* .... ❍Yes ❍No ❍?
...through the means/ways of *the Holy Spirit* .... ❍Yes ❍No ❍?

19❑ As you study this book, pay attention to insight into Jonah's personality. It will help you consider how and why he reacts and responds as he does (which may help you develop a hypothesis).

By whatever means, God's word caused Jonah's mind to think and pay attention to His command................................ ❍True ❍False ❍?

The goal of this work-in-a-book, *aka* workbook, is to teach in any way that helps you understand and retain the information to put into practice the word of God, *aka:* "practical application."

Beginning in the 1950s, educators and researchers developed models and representations of how we retain information taught. Here is a "learning pyramid" attributed to American educator Edward Dale (1900–1985). In general, people remember:

10% of
what they **READ**

20% of what they **HEAR**

30% of what they **SEE**

50% of what they **HEAR** & **SEE**

70% of what they **SAY** & **WRITE**

90% of what they **DO**

20❑ To help you slow down in reading to retain more, you are encouraged to write out the scripture of focus. And, to help you notice details, at every English grammar punctuation mark/symbol start a new line of writing. With the exception of and apostrophe', you will look for the other fifteen (15) marks as listed: period**.** comma**,** question mark**?** exclamation point**!** semicolon**;** colon**:** em dash**—** en dash**–** hyphen- parentheses **( )** bracket **[ ]** brace **{ }** "quotation marks" single quotation mark' and ellipsis**...** The first verse is done for you:

Jonah 1:1 Now the word of the Lord came to Jonah the son of Amittai, saying,

Now the word of the Lord came to

Jonah the son of Amittai,

saying,

Jonah 1:2 Arise, go to Nineveh, that great city, and cry against it; for their wickedness is come up before me.

1❑ Handwrite Jonah 1:2. As the previous example shows (pg ***64***), when the sentence is long, indent the next line as you continue. Remember to start on a new line after each punctuation mark. ▲

▲ *Note: Biblical Hebrew does not contain lower-case letters or punctuation. Punctuation marks were added when scrolls written in Hebrew were* ***transliterated*** *[the conversion of the alphabet of one language to another] to English to help readers understand the structure of the sentence, to clarify or convey the feeling, meaning, or tone the writer intended, to cause us to notice subtle degrees of differences, figures of speech, and assist interpretation.*

2❑ Verse 1:2 contains a list of commands from God; what are they?

1 __________

2 __________

3 __________

3❑ What is the most challenging thing you have ever believed God wanted you to do?

☆ It would be nice to talk with someone about this subject.

4❑ The word **Arise** H6965 is a *verb*, [a part of speech that expresses action, motion, being, suffering, or a request or command to do or forbear anything]. Here is the definition extended for clarity:

❍1 ..Arise, [after lying down], *as in get up.*
❍2 ... Arise [out of your condition, state, circumstances]
❍3 ..... Arise, [move]
❍4 ....Arise, [become powerful]
❍5 .... Arise, [come on the scene]
❍6 .... Arise, [stand]
❍7 ....Arise, [be established]
❍8 .... Arise, [endure]
❍9 .... Arise, [persist]

Mark all the definitions that could reasonably apply to God's directive within the context of Jonah 1:1–2.

5❑ Jonah is told to take action, first **arise**, then _ _ [v walk; depart; proceed; move].

Jonah was told to go to Nineveh **...that great** [H1419 *adj* going beyond, surpassing, excelling, outdoing, great in extent, quality, or duration; superabundant in magnitude and extent] **city...**

Your guess, Nineveh is: ❑ big/vast/spacious ❑ important/significant.

6❑ At the time of Jonah (✍785–760 BC), Nineveh was a city within Assyria. Assyria is first mentioned in the account of Adam and Eve in the Garden of Eden. Circle the word Assyria in the text below:

> *Genesis 2:8–14* (✍1445–1405 BC) *8* **And the Lord God planted a garden eastward in Eden; and there he put the man whom he had formed.** *9* **And out of the ground made the Lord God to grow every tree that is pleasant to the sight, and good for food; the tree of life also in the midst of the garden, and the tree of knowledge of good and evil.** *10* **And a river went out of Eden to**

water the garden; and from there it was parted, and became into four heads. *11* **The name of the first is** *Pison*: **that is it which compasses the whole land of Havilah, where there is gold;** *12* **And the gold of that land is good: there is bdellium and the onyx stone.** *13* **And the name of the second river is** *Gihon*: **the same is it that compasses the whole land of Ethiopia.** *14* **And the name of the third river is** *Hiddekel (aka: Tigris†)*: **that is it which goes toward the east of Assyria. And the fourth river is** *Euphrates*.

†Added for clarity

The Tigris River was also known as *(aka)*: _ _ _ _ _ _ _ _

The approximate location of the ●Tigris and ■Euphrates river today:

7❑ Draw a dark outline around the country of Israel to make it obvious on the map.

8❑ The State of Israel measures about 260 miles/420 km in length and 72 miles/115 km across at its widest point (8,360 square miles). It most closely compares in size to this U.S. state:

❍ Delaware 1,950 ❍ New Hampshire 8,952 ❍ New Jersey 7,354

9❑ This map shows an estimate of the expanse of Assyrian invasions over thousands of years (circled) and the location of Nineveh✖ at the time of Jonah. ❑ Draw a line from this point to Nineveh✖.

Which country is Nineveh located in today? _ _ _ _

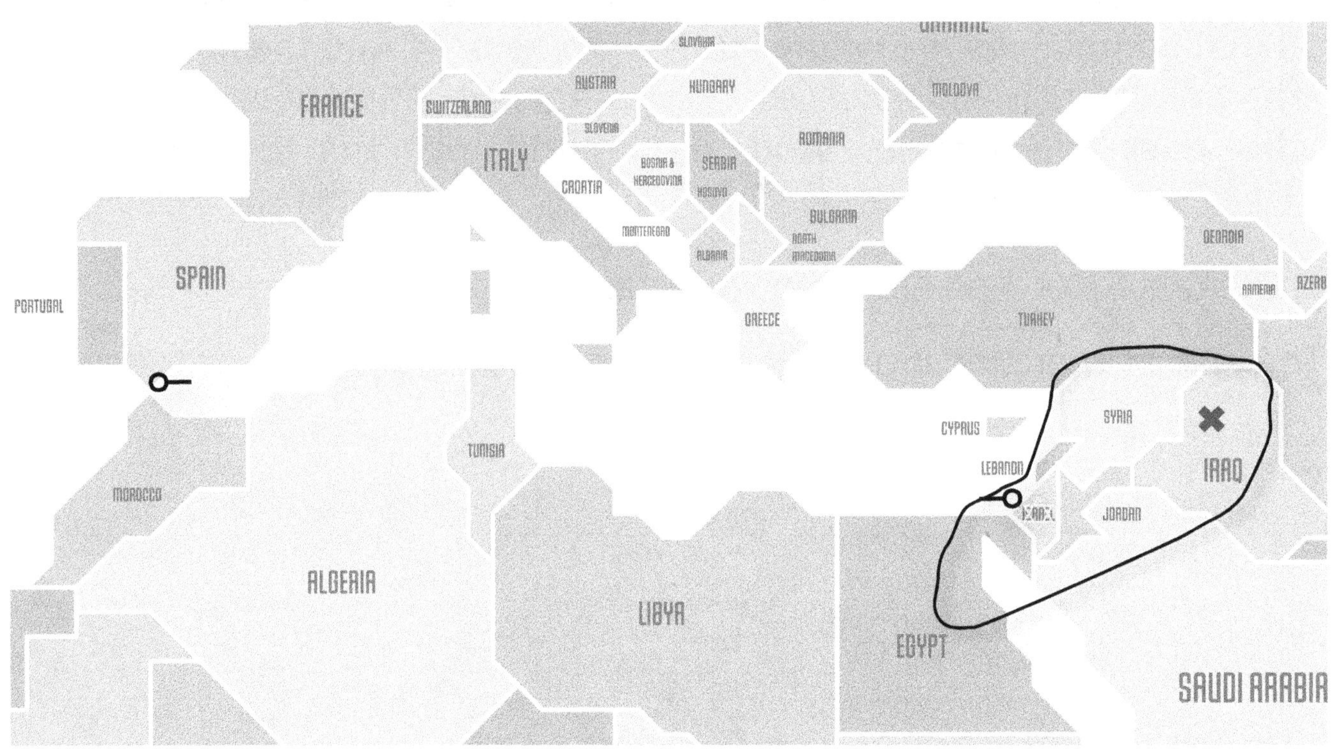

10❑ Using the world map beginning on page **72**. Locate the following and mark each in a unique way (shape, icon, symbol, highlight, etc.). ❍ Iraq ❍ Israel ❍ Spain ❍ Your present location

11❑ Using the same map, which countries border Israel?

❍ **A:** Africa, Iraq, Spain, Turkey
❍ **B:** China, Italy, Russia, Saudi Arabia
❍ **C:** Egypt, Jordan, Lebanon, Syria

12❑ Using the same map, which large body of water borders Israel?

❍ **A:** Black Sea
❍ **B:** Mediterranean Sea
❍ **C:** Red Sea

Arctic Circle
Beaufort Sea
ARCTIC
Ellesmere Island
Queen Elizabeth Islands
Victoria Island
Bering Sea
Alaska (US)
Baffin Bay
Greenland (Dk.)
Greenland Sea
Baffin Island
Norwegian Sea
Gulf of Alaska
Hudson Bay
ICELAND
CANADA
PACIFIC
OCEAN
Newfoundland
ATLANTIC
OCEAN
UNITED STATES
UNITED KINGDOM
North Sea
IRELAND
FRANCE
Gulf of Biscaya
PORTUGAL
SPAIN
Mediterranean
MEXICO
Gulf of Mexico
Cancer
Bahamas
MOROCCO
ALGERIA
WESTERN SAHARA
CUBA
HAITI
DOM. REP.
JAMAICA
BELIZE
HONDURAS
GUATEMALA
EL SALVADOR
NICARAGUA
Carribean Sea
COSTA RICA
PANAMA
VENEZUELA
COLOMBIA
GUYANA
SURINAM
FR. GUYANA
MAURITANIA
MALI
SENEGAL
CAPE VERDE
GUINEA BISSAU
GUINEA
BURKINA FASO
SIERRA LEONE
LIBERIA
COTE d'IVOIRE
GHANA
TOGO
BENIN
Gulf of Guinea
SAO TOME & PRINCIPE
Equator
Galapagos-Islands (Ec.)
ECUADOR
PERU
BRAZIL
Ascension
ATLANTIC
St. Helena
BOLIVIA
FRENCH POLYNESIA
PACIFIC
PARAGUAY
Pitcairn (GB)
Easter Island (Ch.)
ARGENTINA
OCEAN
CHILE
URUGUAY
OCEAN
Tristan da Cunha
Falkland Islands (GB)
South Georgia (GB)

World map

OCEAN
Severnaya Zemlya
Novosibirskie Ostrova
Zemlya Franca-Josifa
Barents Sea
Nowaya Zemlya
Bering Sea
Sea of Ochotsk
RUSSIA
FINLAND
ESTONIA
LATVIA
LITHUANIA
BELARUS
UKRAINE
PACIFIC
KAZAKHSTAN
MONGOLIA
East Sea (Sea of Japan)
JAPAN
NORTH KOREA
SOUTH KOREA
ROMANIA
SERBIA
GEORGIA
ARMENIA
AZERB.
Caspian Sea
Black Sea
UZBEKISTAN
KYRGYSTAN
TURKMENISTAN
TADSCHIKISTAN
OCEAN
TURKEY
GREECE
SYRIA
CYPRUS
LEBANON
IRAQ
ISRAEL
JORDAN
IRAN
AFGHANISTAN
CHINA
East China Sea
Tropic of C
KUWAIT
SAUDI ARABIA
BAHRAIN
QATAR
U.A.E.
PAKISTAN
NEPAL
BHUTAN
INDIA
BANGLADESH
MYANMAR (BURMA)
Taiwan
LIBYA
EGYPT
OMAN
LAOS
Hainan
Arabian Sea
Bay of Bengal
THAILAND
VIETNAM
CAMBODIA
PHILIPPINES
Northern Mariana Islands (US)
Guam (US)
CHAD
SUDAN
Red Sea
YEMEN
ERITREA
DJIBOUTI
Adaman Sea
South China Sea
CENTRAL-AFRICAN REP.
SOUTH SUDAN
ETHIOPIA
SOMALIA
SRI LANKA
MALDIVES
BRUNEI
Celebes Sea
PALAU
FEDERATED STATES OF MICRONESIA
MARSHALL IS.
UGANDA
KENYA
MALAYSIA
Kalimantan (Borneo)
Sumatra
Sulawesi
DEMOCR. REP. OF THE CONGO
RWANDA
BURUNDI
SEYCHELLES
Equator
NAURU
TANZANIA
INDONESIA
Banda Sea
INDIAN
PAPUA NEW GUINEA
Solomon Sea
SOLOMON ISLANDS
ANGOLA
ZAMBIA
MALAWI
COMOROS
TIMOR-LESTE
Timor Sea
MADAGASCAR
NAMIBIA
ZIMBABWE
MOZAMBIQUE
MAURITIUS
Reunion (Fr.)
BOTSWANA
Coral Sea
VANUATU
OCEAN
SWAZILAND
LESOTHO
SOUTH AFRICA
New Caledonia (Fr.)
AUSTRALIA
Tropic
South Australian Basin
Tasman Sea
Tasmania
NEW ZEALAND

13❑ Circle the word ❍ Asshur in the following **genealogy** [race+kind; an account or history of the descent of a person or family from an ancestor; the act of naming ancestors and their children in the natural order of succession; pedigree; lineage]:

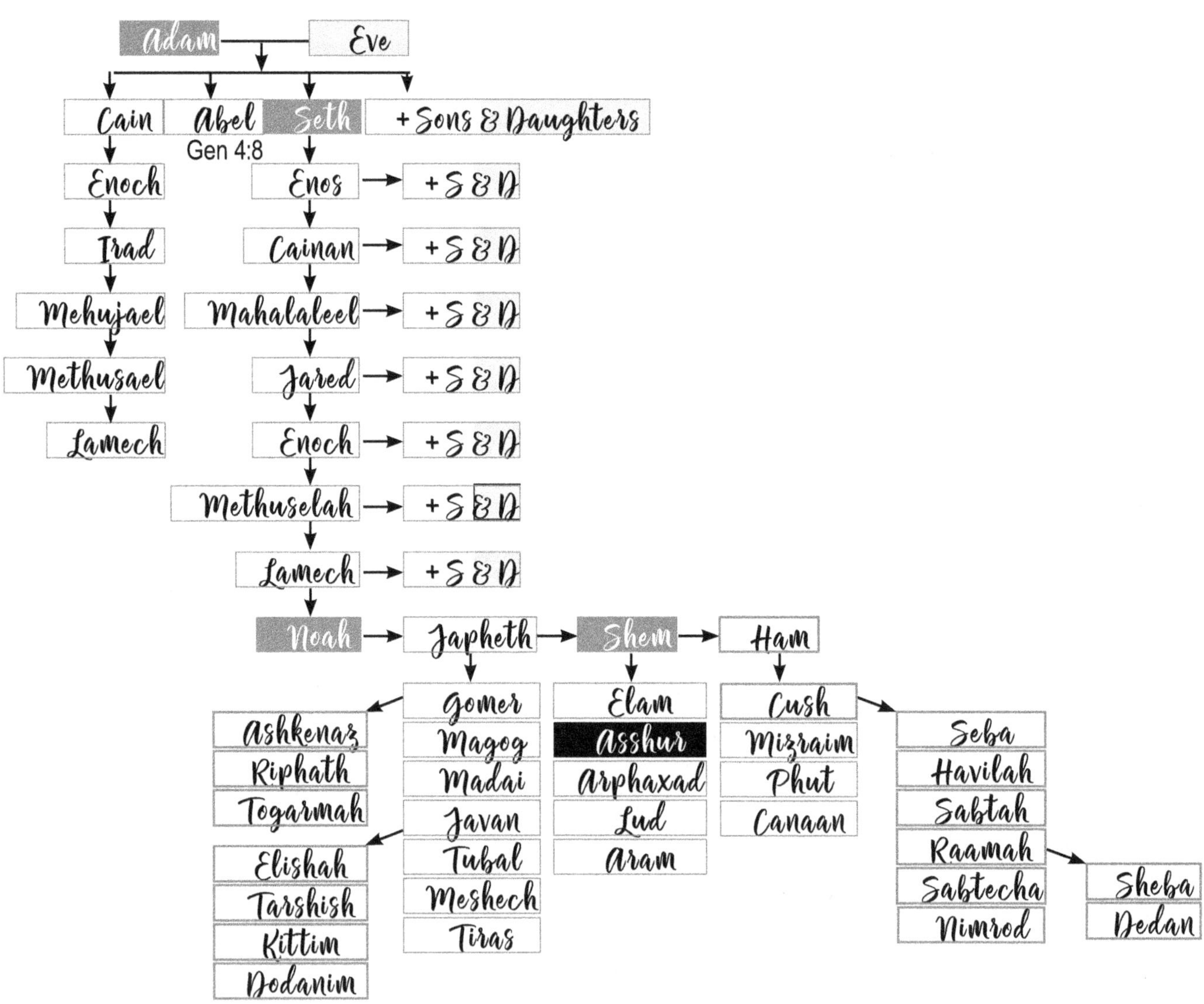

14❑ Asshur's father is: _ _ _ _

Asshur's grandfather is: _ _ _ _

Asshur's great-grandfather is: _ _ _ _

Asshur's great-great-grandfather is: _ _ _ _

15❑ Circle the words ❍ Nineveh and ❍ Asshur in the following verse:

Genesis 10:1—12 (✍1445—1405 BC) **Now these are the generations**
of the sons of Noah, Shem, Ham, and Japheth: and to them were
sons born after the flood. *2* **The sons of Japheth; Gomer, and**
Magog, and Madai, and Javan, and Tubal, and Meshech, and
Tiras. *3* **And the sons of Gomer; Ashkenaz, and Riphath, and**
Togarmah. *4* **And the sons of Javan; Elishah, and Tarshish, Kittim,**
and Dodanim. *5* **By these were the isles of the Gentiles divided**
in their lands; every one after his tongue, after their families, in
their nations. *6* **And the sons of Ham; Cush, and Mizraim, and**
Phut, and Canaan. *7* **And the sons of Cush; Seba, and Havilah,**
and Sabtah, and Raamah, and Sabtecha: and the sons of Raamah;
Sheba, and Dedan. *8* **And Cush begat Nimrod: he began to be a**
mighty one in the earth. *9* **He was a mighty hunter before the**
LORD: wherefore it is said, Even as Nimrod the mighty hunter
before the LORD. *10* **And the beginning of his kingdom was Babel,**
and Erech, and Accad, and Calneh, in the land of Shinar. *11* **Out**
of that land went forth Asshur, and builded Nineveh, and the city
Rehoboth, and Calah, *12* **And Resen between Nineveh and Calah:**
the same is a great city.

16❑ Who built/established the city of Nineveh? ____________________

17❑ **Asshur** *Assyria, Assyrian(s), Assur* [H804 'aššûr *ash-***shoor** n from H833 (in the sense of successful); the second son of Shem; also his descendants and the country occupied by them (i.e., Assyria), its region and its empire which included Babylonia and Mesopotamia; the people of Asshur (an invading army and world-power); builder of Nineveh, Rehoboth, Calah, and Resen].

The land of Asshur and the country of Assyria
are one and the same .... ❍T ❍F ❍?

Assyrians are of the lineage/genealogy of Adam & Eve .... ❍T ❍F ❍?

18❑ It is estimated Jonah was written, and the events occurred between 785—760 BC. Nineveh became Assyria's capital during King Sennacherib's reign 705—681 BC. Was Nineveh the capital city during the time of Jonah? .... ❍Yes ❍No ❍?

19❑ 1:2 Let's focus on the details of **that great city** [a place guarded by a watch; fortified; oppressive bloody city].

Watch v [to guard from error and danger; have in keeping; observe in ambush; lie in wait for; to tend; observe to detect or prevent, or for some particular purpose]
Fortified v [to surround with a wall, ditch, palisades or other works to defend against the attacks of an enemy; to strengthen and secure by forts; to strengthen against any attack; to confirm; to add strength and firmness to; to furnish with strength or means of resisting force, violence or assault]
Oppressive *adj* [unreasonably burdensome; unjustly severe; tyrannical (unjust exercise of power in government); overpowering; overwhelming
Bloody *adj* [stained with blood; murderous; given to the shedding of blood; or having a cruel, savage (wild; untamed; uncivilized disposition)]

Based on Jonah 1:2 and the above definitions, the city of Nineveh and its inhabitants (the Ninevites) might be known for:

____

____

____

20❑ God wanted Jonah to speak against Nineveh **for** [H358 kî *kee* *conj* yea indeed that; because, since; but rather; so that, in order that; at that time; which; surely; forasmuch as] **their** _ _ _ _ _ _ _ _ _ _ _ **is come up** [H5927 'ālâ *aw-**law*** v to bring up; cause to ascend or go up; bring against; rouse, stir up mentally] **before me** [H6440 pānîm *paw-**neem'*** *n* the face (the part turned towards anyone); to say or do anything to anyone's face, in front of]**.**

21❑ There are over six-hundred-sixty-six (660) uses of H7451 **wickedness** in the Bible, nine (9) in the Book of Jonah.

wickedness [H7451 ra' *rrah* n evil manner of thinking and acting; injurious, having qualities which tend to injury or produce mischief; that which is displeasing to God and anyone; noxious, hurtful; sad of heart or mind; badness especially in an ethical sense; malignant; unpleasant, giving pain, unhappiness, misery; vicious in disposition or temper; bad, evil, wicked of persons, thoughts, deeds, or actions; corrupt; perverse; producing sorrow, distress, injury, or calamity].

Using the Book of Jonah printouts (page **7**), draw a pitchfork over the words used for wickedness:

❍ Jonah 1:2 (wickedness) ❍ 1:7 (evil) ❍ 1:8 (evil) ❍ 3:8 (evil)
❍ 3:10 (evil) ❑ 4:1 (exceedingly) ❍ 4:2 (evil) ❍ 4:6 (grief)

22❑ Wickedness/evil begins in the mind?...... ❍Agree ❍Disagree ❍?

23❑ Evil thoughts *do not* tend/move/lead to evil actions .. ❍T ❍F ❍?

24❑ Next, you will find **cross-reference** [refers to related information in another part of the Bible] scripture addresses. If possible, find each of the verse(s) in your Bible (or ask to borrow one), and do one or more of the following *suggestions*:

a) Read the *entire chapter* to understand the **context** [what comes before and after the verse or passages],
b) Read the *paragraph* the verse appears in,
c) Read at least one verse *before and after*,
d) Read just the verse(s) referenced,
e) Make notes to highlight anything you find helpful, interesting, or want to share with others,
f) Handwrite (lines provided) *all or portions* to hide God's word in your heart like King David: **Your word have I hid in my heart, that I might not sin against you.** *Psalm 119:11*

❍ Genesis 6:5 (✍1415–1410 BC) ❍ Before ❍ During ❍ After Jonah

❍ Jeremiah 17:9–10 (✍627–586 BC) ❍ Before ❍ During ❍ After Jonah

❍ Mark 7:20–23 (✍AD 55–65) ❍ Before ❍ During ❍ After Jonah

Mark 7:20—23 (continued) ____________________

25❑ God knows <u>our</u> **manner** [form; method; a way of performing or executing; custom; habitual practice; peculiar way; distinct mode] **of**
❍ **action** [literally, a driving; hence, the state of acting or moving; the exertion of power or force; a thing done; a deed; conduct; behavior; demeanor]
❍ **thought** [properly, that which the mind thinks, either the act or operation of the mind; idea; conception; reflection; opinion or judgment; meditation; serious consideration; inward reasoning; the workings of conscience (internal or self-knowledge, or judgment of right and wrong)].

❍ If you have been **prompted** [ready and quick to act as occasion demands] in your heart of any bad actions or thoughts, *"talk to God"* (pray) in your heart/mind or on paper. *Confession is a mind healer!*

☆ It would be nice to talk with someone about this subject.

Jonah 1:3 But Jonah rose up to flee to Tarshish from the presence of the Lord, and went down to Joppa; and he found a ship going to Tarshish: so he paid the fare thereof, and went down into it, to go with them to Tarshish from the presence of the Lord.

1❑ Handwrite Jonah 1:3. When a sentence is long, indent the next line as you continue. Remember to start on a new line after each punctuation mark (see page ***64***).

2❑ The Lord gave specific commands. What was Jonah's response?

God's Command: **Jonah's action/response**:

A) Arise ____________

B) Go to Nineveh ____________

C) Cry against it ____________

3❑ "Jonah obeyed the first command" is debatable?........... ✓T ❍F ❍?

4❑ The phrase **rose up** is interesting. It means: [H6965 qûm *koom* v after lying down, or out of a condition, make a move; become powerful; come on the scene; stand, to be established, endure, persist]

5❑ Is it *possible* Jonah... was asleep? .... ❍Yes ❍No ❍?

...was prone to laziness? .... ❍Yes ❍No ❍?

...may have been in a depressed condition? .... ❍Yes ❍No ❍?

...may have been a procrastinator?............................. ❍Yes ❍No ❍?

...lacked motivation or purpose?................................ ❍Yes ❍No ❍?

...was weak in strength of character?......................... ❍Yes ❍No ❍?

...needed confidence?.. ❍Yes ❍No ❍?

...was a quitter seeking an "easy out"? .... ❍Yes ❍No ❍?

I can defend my answer based on: ❍ doctrine ❍ fact ❍ feeling ❍ guess ❍ hypothesis ❍ investigation ❍ judgment ❍ opinion ❍ Scripture ❍ theology ❍ theory (definitions pg ***61—62***). ☆ Worthy of discussion.

Scripture/address: ______________________________

6❑ The word **flee** [H1272 bārah *bah-**rakh*** v to pass or cut through; bolt; make haste; run away; put to flight] communicates the sense of a quick decisive action. A **synonym** [similar word] is **escape** [to flee from and avoid; evade].

Is there evidence Jonah gave God's command much consideration, meditation, prayer, or thought?.................................. ❍Yes ❍No ❍?

When circumstances don't go according to your hopes or plans, might you be guilty of making quick decisions that are ultimately not in your best interest? .... ❍Yes ❍No ❍?

7❑ Most biblical scholars believe **Tarshish** [H8659 taršîš *tairr-**sheesh*** Proper noun] *(not to be confused with the name of a descendant of Noah)* was located on the south coast of Spain. It was a commercial

seaport [a city or town situated on a harbor] of the Mediterranean Sea. A harbor is a port, bay, cove, recess, or inlet of the sea in which ships can drop an anchor or ride in safety to shelter from the fury of rough wind and water.

A merchant is one who travels about to foreign countries to trade money or goods for possessions or one who exports and imports goods and sells them as a pedlar. Kings employed merchants to make journeys to other lands to purchase movable objects of commerce such as goods/wares, supplies, and unique things.

❍ Make a list of the items of **import** [merchandise *brought into* a country from another] and/or **export** [merchandise *transported to* a country from another] found in the following scriptures:

2 Chronicles 9:21 (✍430 BC) **For the king's ships went to Tarshish with the servants of Huram: every three years once came the ships of Tarshish bringing gold, and silver, ivory, and apes, and peacocks.**

Ezekiel 27:12 (✍571 BC) **Tarshish was your merchant by reason of the multitude of all kind of riches; with silver, iron, tin, and lead, they traded in your fairs.**

____

____

____

8❏ What is the value or purpose of imports/exports

Imports:____

____

Exports:____

____

◁ ◁ ◁ PAUSE Jonah 1:3

A❑ The Bible teaches three truths described by words you may not be familiar with: Omnipotent, Omnipresent, and Omniscient

1 God is omnipotent *aam-**ni**-puh-tnt* [Almighty G7451 *n* the all-ruling, God as absolute and universal sovereign; he who holds sway over all things *adj* [almighty; possessing unlimited power; all-powerful; having unlimited power of a particular kind].

In the verses below, underline the words ❍ *Almighty*, ❍ *omnipotent* :

Revelation 1:8 (✍AD 90—95) **I am Alpha and Omega, the beginning and the ending, saith the Lord, which is, and which was, and which is to come, the Almighty.**

Revelation 19:6 (✍AD 90—95) **And I heard as it were the voice of a great multitude, and as the voice of many waters, and as the voice of mighty thunderings, saying, Alleluia: for the Lord God omnipotent reigns.**

❍ Briefly describe your understanding of the word omnipotent:

____

____

2 God is omnipresent *aam-nuh-**preh**-znt* *adj* [present in all places at the same time (simultaneously); ubiquitary (existing everywhere, or in all places); He exists through space, speed, and darkness. God is Spirit (not an impersonal "force")] **"God is Spirit: and they that worship him must worship him in spirit and in truth."** *John 4:24* In the verses that follow underline the words ❍ *present*, ❍ *presence*, ❍ *every place* :

Psalm 46:1 (✍799–700 BC) **God is our refuge and strength, a very** *present* **help in trouble.**

Psalm 139:7–12 (✍1000–900 BC) *7* **Where shall I go from your spirit? or where shall I flee from your presence?** *8* **If I ascend up into heaven, you are there: if I make my bed in hell, behold, you are there.** *9* **If I take the wings of the morning, and dwell in the uttermost parts of the sea;** *10* **Even there shall your hand lead me, and your right hand shall hold me.** *11* **If I say, Surely the darkness shall cover me; even the night shall be light about me.** *12* **Yea, the darkness hides not from you; but the night shines as the day: the darkness and the light are both alike to you.**

Proverbs 15:3 (✍1000–900 BC) **The eyes of the Lord are in every place, beholding the evil and the good.**

Jeremiah 23:23–24 (✍627–586 BC) **Am I a God at hand, says the Lord, and not a God afar off?** *24* **Can any hide himself in secret places that I shall not see him? says the Lord. Do not I fill heaven and earth? says the Lord.**

❍ Briefly describe your understanding of the word omnipresent:

____

____

3 God is omniscient *aam-***ni***-shnt* n [having universal knowledge or knowledge of all things; infinitely knowing; all-seeing.

God's omniscience *aam-***ni***-shns* n [the quality of knowing all things at once; universal knowledge; knowledge unbounded or infinite. Omniscience is an attribute peculiar (that which belongs to a person in exclusion of others) to God]

❍ Briefly describe your understanding of the word omniscient:

____

____

____

In the verses that follow, underline the words ❍ *know,* ❍ *beholds all,* ❍ *looks upon all,* ❍ *knows all,* ❍ *all my ways* :

1 Kings 8:39 (✍586–539 BC) **Then hear you in heaven your dwelling place, and forgive, and do, and give to every man according to his ways, whose heart you know; (for you, even you only, know the hearts of all the children of men;)**

Psalm 33:13–14 (✍1000–900 BC) **The Lord looks from heaven; he beholds all the sons of men.** *14* **From the place of his habitation he looks upon all the inhabitants of the earth.**

1 John 3:20 (✍AD 80–85) **For if our heart condemn us, God is greater than our heart, and knows all things.**

Psalm 139:1–4 (✍1000–900 BC) *1* **O LORD, you have searched me, and known me.** *2* **You know my downsitting and my uprising, you understand my thought afar off.** *3* **You compass my path and my lying down, and are acquainted with all my ways** *4* **For there is not a word in my tongue, but, lo, O LORD, you know it altogether.**

B❑ Draw a line to match the left word bubble to its brief definition:

Omni**potent** ❍ ❍ knowledge of all things

Omni**present** ❍ ❍ all-ruling, absolute universal sovereign power

Omni**science** ❍ ❍ exists everywhere at all times

C❑ List some things God cannot do:

____

____

____

____

____

▷ ▷ ▷ PERSEVERE Jonah 1:3

9❑ It is *possible* to **flee** [H1272 v to pass or cut through; bolt; make haste; run away; put to flight] **from the presence** [H6440 n the face (the part turned towards anyone); the face as the surface or front of a thing; from before, in front of] **of the Lord,** [Yehôvâh *yeh-ho-**vaw*** [YHWH H3068 n the existing One, self-Existent Eternal]. ....❍Agree ❍Disagree ❍?

I can defend my answer based on: ❍ doctrine ❍ fact ❍ feeling ❍ guess ❍ hypothesis ❍ investigation ❍ judgment ❍ opinion ❍ Scripture ❍ theology ❍ theory (definitions pg ***61–62***). ☆ Worthy of discussion.

*Scripture/address:*____

10❑ Look at the map on page ***70***. If you look closely at the country of Israel, you will see a circle-line icon smaller than this: **—O** And another located at the southern tip of Spain like this: **O—**

❍ Connect the circle-line icon from Israel to Spain.

11❑ The span from Joppa, Israel (modern day Tel Aviv) to Tarshish (modern-day Gibraltar a British Overseas Territory on Spain's south coast) is estimated to be over 2,300 miles/3698 km "as a bird flies."
❍ Write 2,300 miles/3698 km above the icon line drawn earlier.

12❑ Draw a different line connecting Israel **—O** to Nineveh, ✖ Assyria (modern-day Mosul, Iraq). ❍ Write 600 miles/900 km above that line to represent its distance.

Calculate 2,300 less 600. How many miles difference is it? _ _ _ _

Which location is closest to Joppa, Israel? .....❍ Nineveh ❍ Tarshish
What is the best mode of travel to Tarshish? ...❍ by ship ❍ by land
What is the best mode of travel to Nineveh? ....❍ by ship ❍ by land

13❑ What did Jonah believe would happen if he fled to Tarshish?

____

____

14❑ Have you ever allowed yourself to be deluded/deceived/misled by a pressing decision? .... ❍Yes ❍No ❍?

15❑ Have you ever attempted to explain or justify your attitude or behavior even though it wasn't appropriate, logical, reasonable, right, or true? .... ❍Yes ❍No ❍?

16❑ Read the definition of **from the presence** [H6440 *n* the face (the part turned towards anyone); to turn oneself in any direction; to say or do anything to anyone's face, freely, frankly, and even often impudently (shamelessly with indecent assurance accompanied with a disregard of the opinions of others, lacking modesty, bold with contempt of others) and insolently (proud, haughty, rude, overbearing; domineering) in contempt (despising, viewing, considering, and treating others as worthless); to look on anyone with an angry countenance; to pour out one's anger against anyone; the face as the surface or front of a thing; from before, in front of].

Notice how personal "presence" is. It refers to the face. Jonah thought he could somehow escape God's notice, care and concern. The definition also gives a sense of an *"in your face"* attitude.

What *might* describe Jonah's manner of behaving/feeling/thinking?

____

____

____

____

____

 PAUSE Jonah 1:3

A❑ Events, circumstances, and situations cause reactions in our body and mind. The following is a progression we navigate daily:

1a EMOTION—Involuntary [not proceeding from choice or done willingly] Unpredictable God-given natural emotions affect the body, which moves or agitates your mind to **excite** [to rouse, call into action, animate, stir up, stimulate; to give new or increased action to] your perception of what is occurring.

1b Intentional EMOTION—Voluntary [acting by choice or free will without being impelled, influenced, or restrained by another]
A person's free will choice of deliberate **conscious** [possessing the faculty or power of knowing one's own thoughts or mental operations] thought or attention in response to something unexpected.

❍ Involuntary emotions are generally predictable. .... ❍T ❍F ❍?

2 FEELING—*your response to emotion(s)*

Mindful [regarding with care; bearing in mind; heedful; observant] **awareness** [expecting an event from information or probability] that you will either **suffer** [to feel or bear what is painful, disagreeable or distressing, either to the body or mind] **pain** [an uneasy sensation in animal bodies, of any degree from slight uneasiness to extreme distress or torture, proceeding from pressure, tension or spasm, separation of parts by violence, or any derangement of functions] or have pleasurable sensations from occurrences of emotion.

❍ It is impossible to manage feelings.............................. ❍T ❍F ❍?

3 PASSION—*results from how you choose to manage feelings*

Passion [a strong driving conviction, desire, enthusiasm, or love which can be used for bad or good purposes and results] proceeds from feelings which produce a reaction to either rejoice/revel/relish in it, or to repel/resist the cause.

❍ Feelings can motivate passion for bad or for good........ ❍T ❍F ❍?

B❑ Checkmark the words *you believe/feel* are <u>involuntary</u> **emotions**:

❍ Admire
❍ Adore
❍ Amused
❍ Anger
❍ Anticipation
❍ Anxiety
❍ Appreciate
❍ Astonished
❍ Awe
❍ Awkward
❍ Benevolence
❍ Bored
❍ Calm
❍ Confused
❍ Craving
❍ Dejection
❍ Delight
❍ Desire
❍ Despair
❍ Devotion
❍ Disgust
❍ Disdain
❍ Empathy
❍ Envy
❍ Excitement
❍ Fear
❍ Grace
❍ Grief
❍ Guilt
❍ Happiness
❍ Hatred
❍ Helpless
❍ Horror
❍ Indignation
❍ Interest
❍ Jealousy
❍ Joy
❍ Love
❍ Mercy
❍ Nostalgia
❍ Pity
❍ Pride
❍ Relief
❍ Romance
❍ Sadness
❍ Satisfaction
❍ Shame
❍ Shyness
❍ Startled
❍ Suffering
❍ Surprise
❍ Trust
❍ Wonder

C❑ Should decisions be made based on feeling(s)? ... ❍Yes ❍No ❍?

D❑ Share one of your ❍ biggest "lesson learned" moments,or ❍ good advice as a result of making a decision based on ❍ involuntary emotion ❍ intentional emotion ❍ feeling ❍ passion.

____

____

____

____

____

____

____

____

☆ It would be nice to talk with someone about this subject.

PERSEVERE Jonah 1:3

17❑ Jonah **went down** [H3381 yārad *yaw-**rad*** v to descend; downward] **to Joppa;** [H330 yāpvô *yaw-**foh*** n seaport shipping capital of Jerusalem (present-day Jaffa/Tel Aviv)]

If Jonah *went down* to Joppa, it *could* mean at that time he was up at his home town, Gath-Hepher, 53 miles/85 km away...... ❍T ❍F ❍?

I can defend my answer based on: ❍ doctrine ❍ fact ❍ feeling ❍ guess ❍ hypothesis ❍ investigation ❍ judgment ❍ opinion ❍ Scripture ❍ theology ❍ theory (definitions pg ***61—62***). ☆ Worthy of discussion.
Scripture/address: ______________________________

No matter where Jonah was when God spoke to his heart/mind, did Jonah had have time to reconsider his decision/actions. . ❍T ❍F ❍?

18❑ 1:3 After Jonah went down to Joppa, what did he do next?

1 ______________________________

2 ______________________________

3 ______________________________

19❑ Jonah found the **ship** [H591 n a vessel adapted to navigation using sails, generally a merchant ship] by ❍ searching ❍ seeking ❍ accident.

20❑ Jonah **paid** [H5414 v equivalent given for services performed] **the fare thereof,** [H7939 n passage price]. That makes him ❑ the **shipmaster** [captain; high ranking] ❑ crew/**mariner**/sailor/shipmate [people who make their living by working on and operating a ship] ❑ a **passenger** [a traveler on a public or private conveyance other than the captain or crew]

21❑ What is Jonah's belief restated at the end of 1:3?

____

22❑ What might you *guess* was Jonah's first emotion or feeling following God's command to go to Nineveh? (see definitions pg ***61***)

____

23❑ Can a person's belief be **misguided** [led astray by evil counsel or wrong direction].. ❍Yes ❍No ❍?

24❑ Can a person be **sincere** [pure; unmixed; being in reality what it appears to be; not feigned; not simulated; not assumed or said for the sake of appearance; real; not hypocritical or pretended] **yet wrong** [one that deviates from rightness of principle or practice prescribed by God; not just or equitable; not right, proper or legal; erroneous; not conforming to truth, or to the rules prescribed for moral conduct, either by divine or human laws]?.. ❍Yes ❍No ❍?

25❑ Share one of your ❍ biggest "lesson learned" moments or ❍ good advice as a result of ❍ being misguided ❍ being sincere yet wrong ❍ trying to hide/flee from the Lord, ❍ ignoring God's command/directive.

____

____

____

____

____

____

____

____

____

☆ It would be nice to talk with someone about this subject.

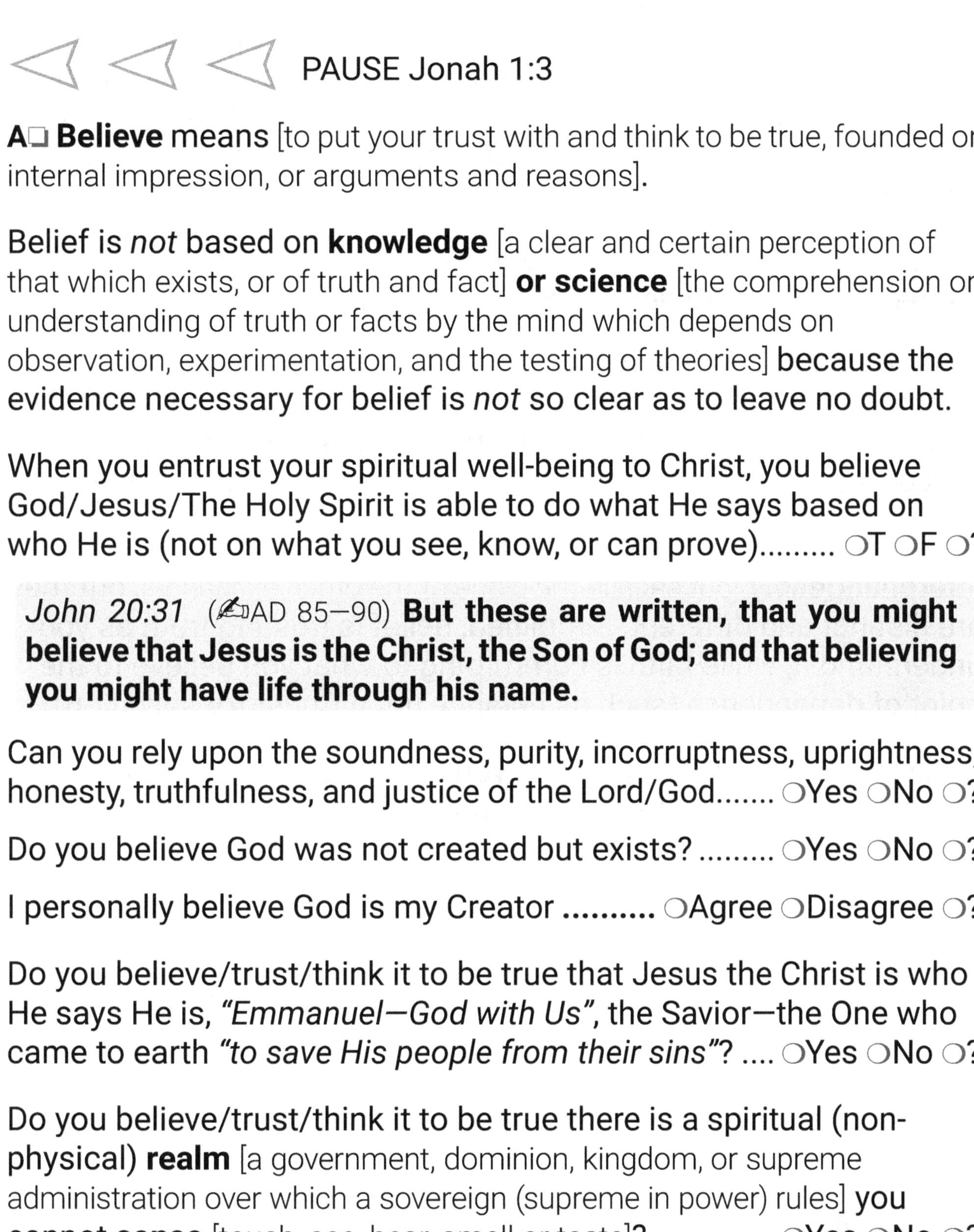

PAUSE Jonah 1:3

A❑ Believe means [to put your trust with and think to be true, founded on internal impression, or arguments and reasons].

Belief is *not* based on **knowledge** [a clear and certain perception of that which exists, or of truth and fact] **or science** [the comprehension or understanding of truth or facts by the mind which depends on observation, experimentation, and the testing of theories] because the evidence necessary for belief is *not* so clear as to leave no doubt.

When you entrust your spiritual well-being to Christ, you believe God/Jesus/The Holy Spirit is able to do what He says based on who He is (not on what you see, know, or can prove)......... ❍T ❍F ❍?

> *John 20:31* (✍AD 85–90) **But these are written, that you might believe that Jesus is the Christ, the Son of God; and that believing you might have life through his name.**

Can you rely upon the soundness, purity, incorruptness, uprightness, honesty, truthfulness, and justice of the Lord/God....... ❍Yes ❍No ❍?

Do you believe God was not created but exists? .... ❍Yes ❍No ❍?

I personally believe God is my Creator .... ❍Agree ❍Disagree ❍?

Do you believe/trust/think it to be true that Jesus the Christ is who He says He is, *"Emmanuel—God with Us"*, the Savior—the One who came to earth *"to save His people from their sins"*? .... ❍Yes ❍No ❍?

Do you believe/trust/think it to be true there is a spiritual (non-physical) **realm** [a government, dominion, kingdom, or supreme administration over which a sovereign (supreme in power) rules] you cannot **sense** [touch, see, hear, smell or taste]?.............. ❍Yes ❍No ❍?

Do you believe what the Bible teaches, that you must be "born again," born spiritually?.. ❍Yes ❍No ❍?

B❑ **Faith** is [a reliance of the mind on the evidence of facts derived from sources other than personal knowledge]. It requires accepting what *another* testifies as truth, resting on *his/her* **integrity** [moral soundness, purity, incorruptness, uprightness and honesty] *without* other evidence.

> *Hebrews 11:1* (✍AD 67–70) **Now faith is the substance of things hoped for, the evidence of things not seen.**

Faith requires **confidence** [reliance in the integrity, stability, or veracity of another, or in the truth and reality of a fact] enough to **commit** [to put into the hands or power of another] to the point of **dependence** [not able to exist or sustain itself without the will, power and operation of another].

Believe and faith are used throughout the Bible somewhat **interchangeably** [put each in the place of the other; exchange], but they are distinct and different. Simplified, belief is trusting truth as you understand it, while faith is committing to what you believe to the point of dependence (such as reliance upon Christ for salvation).

❍ Explain this summarization as you understand it:
Belief isn't doubt-proof—faith isn't reliant upon personal knowledge.

____

____

____

____

____

☆ It would be nice to talk with someone about this subject.

God is truthful and trustworthy.. ❍T ❍F ❍?

I accept evidence and facts from someone I trust............. ❍T ❍F ❍?

Belief is based on trust—Faith is based on dependence.... ❍T ❍F ❍?

C❑ According to the Bible, you must be born again:

John 3:3 (✍AD 85–90) **Jesus answered and said to him, Verily, verily,** [Truly, truly] **I say to you, Except a man be born again,** [from above, a higher place; anew] **he cannot see the kingdom of God.**

If you have been born again/spiritually, when did you do that?

Date/Day: ______________________________

Time/Place: ______________________________

Name of the person who prayed, taught, or shared to lead you:

____

Witness(es), *if any*: ______________________________

Circumstances, experience or testimony: ______________________________

____

____

____

____

____

____

____

____

____

____

☆ It would be nice to talk with someone about this subject.

▷ ▷ ▷ PERSEVERE

Jonah 1:4 But the Lord sent out a great wind into the sea, and there was a mighty tempest in the sea, so that the ship was like to be broken.

1❑ Handwrite Jonah 1:4. When a sentence is long, indent the next line as you continue. Remember to start on a new line after each punctuation mark (page ***64***).

____

____

____

____

____

____

____

2❑ Who controls the weather (atmospheric pressure, blizzard, clouds, drought, hail, cyclone/hurricane/typhoon, ice, rain, sleet, snow, surges, thunderstorms, tornadoes, wind, etc.)?

❍Climate change ❍God/LORD ❍Mankind ❍Mother Nature ❍?

____

I can defend my answer based on: ❍ doctrine ❍ fact ❍ feeling ❍ guess ❍ hypothesis ❍ investigation ❍ judgment ❍ opinion ❍ Scripture ❍ theology ❍ theory (definitions pg ***61—62***). ☆ Worthy of discussion.

Scripture/address: ______________________________

3❑ According to Jonah 1:4, who **sent out** [H2904 v hurled: drive with great force, cast] **a great wind** [H7307 n motion of air]?

❍Climate change ❍God/LORD ❍Mankind ❍Mother Nature ❍?

____

4❑ The word **great** *adjective* is added to the *noun* wind to define and describe the wind as distinctly different. It wasn't an average wind, but **a great** [H1419 *adj* going beyond, surpassing, excelling, outdoing, great in extent, quality, or duration; superabundant in magnitude and extent] wind. What was the result of this wind?

____

5❑ List each definition of **great** (notice the first letter hint):

1 **G** ______________ 3 **E** ______________

2 **S** ______________ 4 **O** ______________

5 **G** ______________

6 **S** ______________

6❑ The **tempest** [H5591 *n* hurricane; storm; whirlwind; used figuratively or as an instrument of God's wrath (anger; indignation)] was **mighty** [H1419 *adj* very strong].

Within the definition, notice the word **figuratively** *adverb* [in a sense different from that which words originally imply, in a manner to exhibit ideas by resemblance. Words are used figuratively when they express something different from their usual or literal meaning].

In keeping with the context of Jonah 1:1–4, do you believe this storm is *"an instrument of God's wrath"* .... ❍Yes ❍No ❍?

7❑ Does the storm seem **supernatural** [beyond or exceeding the powers or laws of nature; miraculous; produced only by the immediate agency of divine (pertaining to the true God) power]? .... ❍Yes ❍No ❍?

I can defend my answer based on: ❍ doctrine ❍ fact ❍ feeling ❍ guess ❍ hypothesis ❍ investigation ❍ judgment ❍ opinion ❍ Scripture ❍ theology ❍ theory (definitions pg ***61—62***). ☆ Worthy of discussion.
Scripture/address: ______________________________

PAUSE Jonah 1:4

The Saffir-Simpson Hurricane Wind scale categorizes storms based on the maximum sustained wind speed. It does not take into account storm surge, rainfall flooding, tornadoes, etc.).

Category 1:	*Winds 74—95 miles per hour (mph)*	*Very dangerous*
Category 2:	*Winds 96—110 mph*	*Extremely dangerous*
Category 3:	*Winds 111—129 mph*	*Devastating*
Category 4:	*Winds 130—156 mph*	*Catastrophic*
Category 5:	*Winds 157 mph or higher*	*Catastrophic*

Beyond wind damage, storm surges account for added loss of life and destruction of land and property. A storm surge (coastal flood) occurs when the seawater level is raised from the wind and, combined with waves, rushes inland to dry land. It is measured at the water level above the normal tidal level, not including waves. *Storm surges account for more deaths than high winds.*

1 On September 2, 1935, the **Labor Day Hurricane** devastated the middle Florida Keys. Winds exceeded 200 mph/321km, storm surges were as high as 18 feet/5.5m), and a 40 mile/64km) wide path of destruction was left as evidence of the most powerful storm to ever reach the United States. It swept a locomotive and more than nine carriages thousands of feet from its tracks. Famed author Earnest Hemingway wrote a piercing, graphic first-hand report on the hurricane. Death toll: 485 Category: 5

2 August 27, 1969: **Hurricane Camille** hit Mississippi and Alabama with winds exceeding 170 mph/273km.

Death toll: 65 Category: 5

3 August 24, 1992: **Hurricane Andrew** reached south Miami-Dade County with winds of 165 mph (265km).

Death toll: 43 Category: 5

4 October 10, 2018: **Hurricane Michael** reached the Florida Panhandle, recording winds over 161 mph/273km.

Death toll: 59 Category: 5

5 On August 29, 2005, **Hurricane Katrina** produced storm surges to 28 feet/8.5m high and traveled 6 to 12 miles/9–19km inland. It made landfall in southeast Louisiana with wind speeds to 127 mph/204km.

Death toll: 1833 Category: 3

A❍ Which storm had the highest maximum sustained wind speed?

B❍ Which storm had the highest loss of life?

C❍ Which storm had the highest storm surge waves?

D❍ What life-threatening **natural disaster** [an event in nature that results in serious damage or death, i.e., earthquake, Tsunami, etc.] have you personally experienced?

With 10 being the most, how life-threatening did it feel to you?

❍1 ❍2 ❍3 ❍4 ❍5 ❍6 ❍7 ❍8 ❍9 ❍10

☆ It would be nice to talk with someone about this subject.

PERSEVERE Jonah 1:4

8❑ During the storm, what was the condition of the **ship** [H591 *n* a vessel adapted to navigation by using sails, generally a merchant ship]?

9❑ According to 1:3, Jonah **went down** [H3381 *v* descended, go downwards, to a lower region] into the ship. Put yourself in *the passenger's* place. What might that experience be like during this storm?

10❑ During a raging sea storm, can a person likely escape from a vessel (abandon ship) and survive? .... ❍Agree ❍Disagree ❍?

11❑ I get **seasick** [affected with sickness or nausea due to the pitching (the rising and falling of the head and stern of a ship, as she moves over waves) or rolling (the motion of a ship from side to side) of a vessel]? .... ❍Always ❍Often ❍Sometimes ❍Never

Roughly one-third of the population experiences motion sickness. Conflicting signals between the inner ear, the eyes, and the movement of your body can cause you to become airsick, carsick, seasick, and/or simulation sick (from virtual reality experiences).

If motion sickness has affected you, mark the ones experienced:

❍ clammy skin ❍ cold sweats ❍ confusion ❍ dehydration ❍ dizziness ❍ drowsiness ❍ flushed face ❍ fatigue ❍ headaches ❍ hyperventilation ❍ increased salivation ❍ lethargy ❍ loss of appetite ❍ nausea ❍ pale skin tone ❍ reduced ability to focus ❍ sensitivity to odors ❍ shallow breathing ❍ vertigo ❍ vomiting ❍ yawning ❍ all of the above

Jonah 1:5 Then the mariners were afraid, and cried every man to his god, and cast forth the wares that were in the ship into the sea, to lighten it of them. But Jonah was gone down into the sides of the ship; and he lay, and was fast asleep.

1❑ Handwrite Jonah 1:5. When a sentence is long, indent the next line as you continue. Remember to start on a new line after each punctuation mark (see page ***64***).

2❑ Mariners are sailors who pilot the sea. **Mariner** [H4419 n sailor (as following "the salt"); seaman; one who navigates or manages vessels in the sea]. Older, experienced sailors earned the nickname "salty" from having been at sea so long.

Sailors had to be strong *and tough!* They were used to cramped quarters, dangers, disease, death, foul weather, hardship, poor pay, and no escape from all types of personalities aboard. Their vessel could sail for months. Life aboard a ship made for a small world.

Someone in difficult living conditions (or a dangerous relationship) might relate or identify with the challenges of a sailor's life.

❍ Share anything you or someone close has experienced that relates to the **hardship** [toil; fatigue; severe labor or want; whatever oppresses the body; injury; oppression; injustice] of a sailor:

With 10 being the most, how hard was the experience?
❍1 ❍2 ❍3 ❍4 ❍5 ❍6 ❍7 ❍8 ❍9 ❍10

3❑ Then the mariners were afraid, [H3372 v fear, be afraid; to stand in awe of; reverence (fear mingled with respect, esteem, and affection); honor: a painful emotion or passion excited by an expectation of evil, or the apprehension of impending danger]

It seems odd that experienced merchant ship sailors were afraid of a storm. .... ❍Agree ❍Disagree ❍?

If you knew the captain and crew of the vessel you boarded were afraid, how might that make you feel?

◁ ◁ ◁ PAUSE Jonah 1:5

Henry Piddington (1797—1858), a British sea captain turned meteorologist, developed a book based on his experiences and that of his brother-sailor's "storm cards." He became an expert on the science of storms on large bodies of water throughout the world.

In "The Sailor's Horn-Book, For the Law of Storms" (1848), Piddington introduced a new word, "**cyclone**," from the Greek word κύκλος (kyklos) meaning [circle, ring, encircling like the coil of a snake.] The word cyclone describes the circular winds of hurricanes, *aka* typhoons or tropical cyclones. **Antiquated** [outdated; obsolete; out of circulation] books like his can give you a sense of how things were, or understood to be, long ago *(though it was written thousands of years after Jonah)*.

A❑ How could Piddington's introduction be applied to your life?

> "…it teaches how to avoid storms,
> how to manage in storms when they cannot be avoided, and
> how to profit by storms!"

____

____

____

____

____

And…

> I know that many (sailors) forget that "a hurricane at sea is like a battle in a campaign; an important, but infrequent occurrence, for which it is wise to be well prepared" and, rarely looking at works like the present till they want assistance from them, are

> thus very liable to mistakes in a moment of anxiety. If such, however, will but give it one fair perusal at leisure, they may perhaps, recollecting with quaint old Thomas Fuller, that "the winds are not only wild in a storm, but even stark mad in a hurricane," find that a little study in fine weather may save a world of labor and mischief in bad.

B❑ Meditate on the wisdom in the above paragraph.

❍ How could you apply it to your time in God's word?

____

____

____

____

____

The following are edited **excerpts** [selected extracts of a writing] from Piddington's book:

The origin of the word "hurricane" is based on superstition:

> This word Hurricane seems originally to have been…speaking of the superstitions of the Indians (Carbis)... "so also when the Devil wishes to terrify them (the Indians), he promises them to Huracan, which means Tempest. ...so fearful to see, that it doubtless appeared to be the Devil's work, and could not be looked on without terror."

C❑ Guess or define your understanding of the word **superstition**:

____

____

The word **religion** can refer to [belief in the being and perfections of God (Yehovah, the self-Existent Eternal), the revelation of His will to man, man's obligation to obey His commands, and man's accountableness to Him], OR

[any system of faith and worship which conceives, contains, implies, or includes the belief and worship of pagans (heathens, Gentiles, non-Jews, idolaters, worshipers of false gods), or of any superior power or powers governing the world].

D❑ Regarding your personal **belief**, [the admission or agreement of your mind to the truth of a declaration, proposition, or alleged fact, on the ground of evidence, distinct from personal knowledge]

❍ I believe God [Yehovah] is the one true God who governs all.

❍ I believe another superior power governs the world.

❍ I believe something else (none of the above).

I can defend my answer based on: ❍ doctrine ❍ fact ❍ feeling ❍ guess ❍ hypothesis ❍ investigation ❍ judgment ❍ opinion ❍ Scripture ❍ theology ❍ theory (definitions pg ***61—62***). ☆ Worthy of discussion.

Scripture/address: ______________________________

Write of your beliefs: ______________________________

____

____

____

____

____

E❑ Who did these 1800s Indians (possibly originating from the Carribean) believe had superior power to govern the weather?

the _ _ _ _ _

F❑ The word **superstition** means: [1) excessive exactness or rigor in religious opinions or practice; extreme and unnecessary scruples in the observance of religious rites not commanded or of points of minor importance; excess or extravagance in religion; the doing of things not required by God, or abstaining from things not forbidden; or the belief of what is absurd, or belief without evidence. 2) superstition has reference to god, to religion, or to beings superior to man. 3) belief in the direct agency of superior powers in certain extraordinary or singular events, or in omens (a remarkable or unusual appearance supposed to indicate something future of good or evil by previous signs) and prognostics (a sign by which a future event may be known or foretold, a foretelling; prediction)].

❍ Write your understanding of superstition after reading the definition:

____

____

____

____

G❑ The Indian's beliefs were based on religion............ ❍Yes ❍No ❍?

Use the definitions on page ***107*** to explain your answer: __________

____

____

Continuing in Piddington's wisdom for sailors:

The inconveniences of major storms:

> …give up the idea of keeping your course.
> …you may have to sacrifice a day to get out of the way of it.
> …(it) blows you all around the compass.
> …drifting hundreds of miles off course.

H❑ Of the "major storms" in your life, such as personal challenges, tragedies, etc., what **idea** [whatever is the immediate object of perception, thought, or understanding in the mind] did you have to let go of:

I❑ What sacrifices did you have to make?

J❑ How did it "blow you all around" and, off course?

Piddington's: Of sights and sounds during dark times:

> ...thunder and lighting are "nearly incessant through the whole of this terrible storm." ...only the very loudest (of thunder) would have any chance of being heard during the height of a hurricane.

K❑ If on a ship in a hurricane, which feels most terrifying?
❍ Breaking of the ship ❍ Heavy rainfall ❍ High waves ❍ Lighting
❍ Loss of ship's power ❍ Rip currents ❍ Strong winds ❍ Thunder

Piddington's examples of the devastation and costly losses:

> …The whole fleet was lost: topmasts, rudders, lower masts, and the entire crew of 400 souls on board.
>
> …upward of three thousand seamen have perished by it. (April 1782)
>
> …when on a sudden, and without the least warning, the vessel was dismasted and sunk by a whirlwind.
>
> …how often do we hear of a dozen of ships putting to sea, of which three or four are never heard of, and three or four return dismasted or otherwise so seriously damaged as to be condemned (or) …sold for a fifth of her insured value.

All hands on deck:

> …some ships…require three or four men at the helm and…will sometimes tear the wheel from their hands and perhaps seriously hurt them if the relieving tackles are not carefully attended to.
>
> ...persons often found on board ships, and who may materially assist us in many things, are the doctors and the passengers.

L❑ Does Piddington's manual give you a sense of danger at sea?
.... ❍Yes ❍No ❍?

The Mediterranean Sea is the ninth (9th) largest sea in the world. Typically, seas are smaller bodies of water than oceans. They begin where land and oceans meet and are partially enclosed by land.

Hurricanes range from 100 to 1000 miles/161–1609km in <u>diameter</u>. They cycle warm, evaporated water from large bodies of water into the air, which releases down through condensation in the form of thunderstorms.

If possible, measure 1,000 miles "as the bird flies" from your present location. For example, if you are from Southern California, Seattle, Washington, is 960 miles/1544km north, Dallas, Texas, is 1,177/1894km east, and Cabo San Lucas is 900 miles/1448km south.

Hurricane Sandy, 2012, had a diameter of 1,150 miles/1850km.

M❑ Can you imagine your location at the center (eye) of a storm extending 500 miles from you in every direction? .... ❍Yes ❍No ❍?

N❑ The following Psalm relates to merchant ships and mariners:

> *Psalm 107:23–31* (✍499–400 BC) *23* **They that go down to the sea in ships, that do business in great waters;** *24* **These see the works of the Lord, and his wonders in the deep.** *25* **For he commands, and raises the stormy wind, which lifts up the waves thereof.** *26* **They mount up to the heaven, they go down again to the depths: their soul is melted because of trouble.** *27* **They reel to and fro, and stagger like a drunken man, and are at their wit's end.** *28* **Then they cry to the Lord in their trouble, and he brings them out of their distresses.** *29* **He makes the storm a calm, so that the waves thereof are still.** *30* **Then are they glad because they be quiet; so he brings them to their desired haven.** *31* **Oh that men would praise the Lord for his goodness, and for his wonderful works to the children of men!**

According to *Psalm 107*, Who is in control of the storm?

____

O❑ What causes those aboard the ship to cry to the Lord?

____

____

____

____

P❑ What melts the soul of a mariner at sea?

Q❑ What would you do before, during, and after a storm?

Before

During

After

PERSEVERE Jonah 1:5

4❑ The mariner's emotions were awakened by fear of impending danger—the change of weather conditions. So afraid they did what?

1 ____________________

2 ____________________

5❑ Have you ever experienced something so alarming that you responded (or panicked) the same way as above? ..... ❍Yes ❍No ❍?

Briefly share your most **similar** [to have the likeness of; equal or close in appearance, degree, figure, form, quality, or quantity] **experience:**

____

____

____

____

____

☆ It would be nice to talk with someone about this subject.

6❑ Faced with alarming danger, whom do you call upon/cry out to?

____

7❑ If surprised or caught off-guard, what would be the first words out of your mouth? *(answer honestly here)*

____

8❑ Ask someone who knows you well, what are they used to hearing you say?

____

 Date: __________

PAUSE Jonah 1:5

A❑ What is God's name? Let's look at what God himself said after He heard the cry of the Egyptian slaves—*the afflicted Israelites*:

> *Exodus 3:13*— (✍1450–1410 BC) *13* **And Moses said to God, Behold, when I come to the children of Israel, and shall say to them, The God of your fathers has sent me to you; and they shall say to me, What is his name? what shall I say to them?** *14* **And God said to Moses, I Am That I Am: and he said, Thus shall you say to the children of Israel, I Am has sent me to you.** *15* **And God said moreover to Moses, Thus shall you say to the children of Israel, the Lord God of your fathers, the God of Abraham, the God of Isaac, and the God of Jacob, has sent me to you: this is my name for ever, and this is my memorial to all generations.**

What did God say his name is (two words): _ _ _

His name, in Hebrew, means he **exists** [H1961 v to be, become; come to pass; exist; happen; occur; come about, come to pass; come into being; to arise, appear].

God was not created. He is the Creator.

> *Genesis 1:1* (✍1450–1410 BC) **In the beginning _ _ _ created the heaven and the earth.**

B❑ You will find many names of God in the Bible. Each reveals His **attributes** [that which is considered as belonging to, inherent, existing in, and inseparable from]. *It is not humanly possible to fully describe God.*

All but a few words in the Old Testament were penned in Hebrew (*aka* Biblical Hebrew). One Hebrew word for God is **Elohim** 'ĕlōhîm *el-o-**heem*** [H430 n 1. specifically used for the Supreme God; the God of Abraham; God of gods; the true God; God of all flesh. 2. It can also be used of a false god, heathen deity (a fabulous god or goddess or being supposed to exist and preside over particular departments of nature), or idol whom some worship in place of God].

יְהֹוָה Two Hebrew names of God

God 'ĕlōhîm [Supreme] God/Lord Yehōvâ [(the) self-Existent]

Notice the word **God** (Elohim) can be used of a _ _ _ _ _ [a sham; deceitful; feigned; liar; not true; not conformable to fact; contrary to what exists] god, a **heathen** [a foreign nation; Gentile; non-Jew] deity, or an **idol** [to resemble; a likeness; figure; an image, form or representation as an object of worship].

When reading and **interpreting** [unfolding what is not understood or obvious; separate one thing from another; understand the differences and judge the meaning of information, words, or actions] references to God as Elohim be careful to apply the correct definition/understanding in **context** [consider the surrounding verses]. It is crucial you determine if the scripture refers to the true God, or a false representation (a god).

Do not rely on whether or not the word begins with a capital letter in English. The Hebrew alphabet does not have a distinction of upper and lowercase letters (nor do the earliest copies of the New Testament in Greek). Modern prints of the Bible, depending upon the one you possess, have been edited to either show every name and pronoun of God to begin with a capital letter, or to leave the words in typical English style (lowercase). The King James Today version retains the KJV non-capitalization style. This Bible study workbook capitalizes the lesson work to make understanding more clear.

C❑ The Hebrew alphabet contains both UPPER and lower case letters. ....❍Correct ❍Incorrect ❍?

D❑ In Hebrew, God (Elohim) sometimes refers to a false god, heathen deity, or idol .... ❍T ❍F ❍?

E❑ In Hebrew, God (Elohim) is used of the Supreme God, the God of Abraham, the God of gods, the true God of all flesh .... ❍T ❍F ❍?

2 Timothy 2:15 **Study to show yourself approved** [acceptable; tried; pleasing] **to God, a workman that needs not to be ashamed, rightly dividing** [handle aright, to teach the truth correctly and directly] **the word of truth.**

F❑ God wants you to read His word and study it further to correctly understand it (to share His truth with others)..................... ❍T ❍F ❍?

The PROBE™ Bible study method steps are:

1) **Pray** it [connect and exchange thoughts with God]

2) **Read** it [understand written words and ideas]

3) **Observe** it [take notice of events, facts, and principles]

4) **Back-it-up** [prove truth]. This is done by **examination** [inquiry into circumstances, facts, and truth], using a variety of resources, i.e., ancient maps, Bible commentaries, concordances, cross-references, dictionaries, encyclopedias, historical documents, interlinear Bibles, lectures, lexicons, teachings, etc. Reliable resources pave the way to a reasonable interpretation. Then you can form an educated **judgment** [the determination of the mind formed from comparing the relations of ideas, or the comparison of facts and arguments to ascertain truth], or **opinion** [the decision the mind forms of truth or falsehood which is supported by a degree of evidence that renders it probable but does not produce absolute knowledge or certainty].

5) **Express** it [make your feelings, opinions, and passions known by your actions, behavior, course of life, leadership, and words]. Respond to God's word as your understanding increases. Acknowledge what you sense God wants you to do. Apply God's word to your life and circumstances. Share personal experiences that bear witness and support what you've learned. Be creative in expressing what God impresses upon your heart. Determine goals, make plans, and evaluate your progress.

G❑ The art of accurately **expounding** [detail a theory or idea; lay open the meaning; clear of obscurity, serving to explain and illustrate] Biblical text requires study in **hermeneutics** [the art of finding the meaning of an author's words and phrases, unfolding the signification through interpreting, and explaining it to others].

❍ Underline the word art used twice in the paragraph above. **Art** is defined as: [skill, dexterity, or the power of performing certain actions acquired by experience, observation or study].

H❑ Using the definition of hermeneutics above, rewrite each part, starting a new line after punctuation marks.

1 ______________________________

____

2 ______________________________

____

3 ______________________________

____

So far, without realizing it, you've worked through PROBE steps 1,2,3, and the first half of 4: 1) **P**ray it 2) **R**ead it 3) **O**bserve it 4) **B**ack-it-up

I❑ To arrive at a reasonable, biblically sound **interpretation** [expounding or unfolding what is not understood or not obvious; to interpret (separate one thing from another; understand the differences and judge the meaning of information, words, or actions)] of Bible passages, you need to exert effort in the discipline of studying.

On the following page, mark the areas of study you would like to:

❍ learn to do ❍ do better ❍ do more of ❍ understand

J❑ This is a brief **A**–to–**Z** list of ***some*** things scholars do and study:

- ❍ **A**NALYSIS
- ❍ **B**IBLICAL CUSTOMS
- ❍ **C**ONTEXT
- ❍ **D**EFINITIONS
- ❍ **E**TYMOLOGY (words)
- ❍ **F**IGURES OF SPEECH
- ❍ **G**RAMMAR
- ❍ **H**ISTORY & LOCATION
- ❍ **I**NTERPRETATION
- ❍ **J**UDAISM
- ❍ **K**INGS & KINGDOMS
- ❍ **L**ITERARY TYPES
- ❍ **M**IRACLES & SIGNS
- ❍ **N**ARRATIVES
- ❍ **O**BSERVATIONS
- ❍ **P**URPOSE
- ❍ **Q**UESTIONING: 5W's+H
- ❍ **R**EPETITION
- ❍ **S**YMBOLISM
- ❍ **T**YPES & ANTITYPE
- ❍ **U**NDERSTANDING PROPHECY
- ❍ **V**ERSE INTEGRITY
- ❍ **W**ORLDVIEW vs BIBLICAL VIEW
- ❍ **X**ERXES & alternate spellings
- ❍ **Y**EARS & SEASONS
- ❍ **Z**EAL in APPLICATION

K❑ Moving forward, there will be times when you form an educated **judgment** [the determination of the mind formed from comparing the relations of ideas or the comparison of facts and arguments to ascertain truth], ***or* opinion** [the decision the mind forms of truth or falsehood which is supported by a degree of evidence that renders it probable but does not produce absolute knowledge or certainty].

❍ Circle the words judgment and opinion above.

Note: Remember to remain humble. It takes education, diligence, resources, time, and wisdom to come to more precise interpretations.

L❑ What is the difference between **reading** [pronouncing or perusing (examining) written or printed words, characters, or letters of a book or writing] and **studying** [a diligent application of the mind or thoughts upon a subject to learn what is not before known]?

____

____

______________________________ ➜

(continued): ______________________________

M❑ What is the difference between judgment and opinion?

N❑ What's the difference between opinion and feeling? (see page ***61***)

O❑ What is the difference between fact and feeling (page ***61***)?

P❑ What is the difference between feelings (page ***61***) and emotions? (page ***89***)

Congratulations! You've progressed beyond simply reading to an in-depth study of God's word. *God is in the details!*

Q❑ What are your thoughts about your progress so far?

R❑ What are some things you've learned?

S❑ The definitions are: ❍ annoying ❍ educational ❍ helpful
T❑ The ◁ PAUSE's are: ❍ annoying ❍ educational ❍ helpful
U❑ So far, this study is: ❍ annoying ❍ educational ❍ helpful
V❑ This study is: ❍ easy ❍ difficult ❍ impossible

PERSEVERE Jonah 1:5

9❑ Go back to page **7** and read to review Jonah 1:1–5. Next, fill in the blanks from the beginning of 1:5:

Then the _ _ _ _ _ _ _ _ _ _ _ **were** _ _ _ _ _ _ _ _ ,

and _ _ _ _ _ _ **every** _ _ _ **to his** _ _ _ **,** 'ĕlōhîm *el-o-**heem*** [H430 *n*]

10❑ How would you apply a definition of Elohim (page ***114***) to the mariner's beliefs? Attempt to **interpret** [separate one thing from another; understand the differences and judge the meaning of information, words, or actions] to whom you sense the seamen called upon/cried out to.

I can defend my answer based on: ❍ doctrine ❍ fact ❍ feeling ❍ guess ❍ hypothesis ❍ investigation ❍ judgment ❍ opinion ❍ Scripture ❍ theology ❍ theory (definitions pg ***61—62***). ☆ Worthy of discussion.

Scripture/address:

11❑ What did they believe regarding this storm?

12❑ What did they believe regarding their safety?

13❑ What did they believe regarding their future?

14❑ To **cast forth** means [H2904 v hurled: drive with great force, cast: to drive from by force, like casting a javelin spear]. Remember, the purpose of a merchant ship is to carry **the wares** [H3627 n articles, utensils, cargo: goods, merchandise, especially things of value] to another location, and ideally, for profit. Hurling the wares overboard would **lighten** [H7043 v make light; reduce in weight; make less heavy] the ship. It was an act of self-preservation. Have you ever been in a situation where you had to let something of value go for a greater purpose? If so share:

15❑ What **consequence(s)** [an event, effect, or series of things produced by some preceding act, cause, condition, principle, or situation, which may be bad or beneficial] **or costs did you incur because of the loss?**

16❑ I can identify with the sailor's fears......... ❍Agree ❍Disagree ❍?

17❑ Who do you think or guess made the decision to toss the goods?

18❑ What might the consequences of lightening the ship be when the vessel and crew reach the intended destination?

19❑ Is it likely the passengers were afraid? .... ❍Y ❍N ❍?
20❑ If you knew the crew was afraid, would you be? .... ❍Y ❍N ❍?

Date: ____________

21❑ Describe your understanding of what the weather must have been like and what it would be like to experience while trying to toss the wares overboard:

22❑ During a historic storm, while sailors were hurling cargo overboard, where was the passenger Jonah, and what was he doing?

23❑ Using the definition of the **sides** [H3411 ɴ the rear or recess: a place of retirement or secrecy; extreme parts] of the ship, what was the purpose or common use of the lower region of the ship?

24❑ Notice in the previous definition, the word **retirement** [the act of withdrawing from company or from public notice or station; the state of being withdrawn; as the retirement of the mind from the senses; private abode; habitation secluded from much society or from public life; private way of life]. In what way(s) does Jonah's plan to flee from the presence of the Lord tie in with his going down into the sides of the ship?

25❑ What would it be like to be **fast asleep** [H7290 v to stun, i.e., stupefy: deprived of sensibility, dull of perception or understanding; be fast in a deep sleep] during all the activity aboard ship:

Put in Jonah's place, would you find sleeping ❍ **easy** [being at rest; free from pain, disturbance or annoyance] ❍ **difficult** [hard to be made, done or performed; attended with labor and pains; not easily managed] ❍ **impossible** [not feasible; that cannot be done; that which is contrary to the law of nature].

26❑ Describe the most ❍ embarrassing ❍ inappropriate ❍ inconvenient ❍ odd or ❍ unusual time/place you've fallen asleep:

Jonah 1:6 So the shipmaster came to him, and said to him, What mean you, O sleeper? arise, call upon your God, if so be that God will think upon us, that we perish not.

1❑ Handwrite Jonah 1:6. When a sentence is long, indent the next line as you continue. Remember to start on a new line after each punctuation mark (see page ***64***).

2❑ The **shipmaster** [H7227 *n* captain, chief officer, head of the sailors; great, large, vast; abundant; strong; a master, one who is skilled in any art] **came to Jonah and questioned him: "what mean** [H4100 *part* what? how? why? when? what! how! for why?] **you** [*prep*]**?"**

Why might the shipmaster be surprised to find Jonah below ship?

3❑ Why might Jonah be surprised to be confronted in his sleep?

4❑ The shipmaster wanted Jonah to explain himself. He calls him **O** _ _ _ _ _ _ _ _ [H7290 v to stun, i.e., stupefy: deprive of sensibility, dull of perception or understanding; be fast in a deep sleep].

5❑ Do you think the shipmaster woke Jonah up?........ ❍Yes ❍No ❍?

6❑ The shipmaster told Jonah: "_ _ _ _ [H7121 v address by name; call out to; preach; publish] **upon** [H413 *prep*] **your God,** *el-o-**heem*** [H430 *n*]".

7❑ Record the two meanings that define **Elohim,** one of the names describing God (see page ***114***):

1

2

8❑ Generally, I am most alert and productive in the:
❍ Morning 6 a.m.–12 p.m. ❍ Afternoon 12 p.m.–6 p.m.
❍ Evening 6 p.m.–12 a.m. ❍ Late night to Early 12 a.m.–6 a.m.

9❑ Re-read verses ❍ 1:5 and ❍ 1:6. Keeping in mind the context (whole sentence, verse, and surrounding verses) and the use of God—Elohim in both, what is a reasonable application of the definition in each verse? *(remember, ignore modern capitalization added by translators)*.

I would apply the Elohim definition part ❍ 1 ❍ 2
to Jonah 1:5 ."...and cried every man to his god..." because:

____

____

I would apply the Elohim definition part ❍ 1 ❍ 2
to Jonah 1:6 "... arise, call upon your God..." because:

____

____

I can defend my answer based on: ❍ doctrine ❍ fact ❍ feeling ❍ guess ❍ hypothesis ❍ investigation ❍ judgment ❍ opinion ❍ Scripture ❍ theology ❍ theory (definitions pg ***61—62***). ☆ Worthy of discussion.
Scripture/address: ________________________________

10❑ In the shipmaster's **plea** [urgent prayer, entreaty, petition, solicitation] to Jonah, he states 1:6: **...if so be** [H194 *adv* if not; perhaps; if so be; peradventure: by chance, perhaps, it maybe, usually expressing a hope] **that God** [H430 *n*] **will** _ _ _ _ _ _ [H6245 v reflect, recollect: bring back to mind; consider] **upon us** [*prep*]...

11❑ Reviewing 1:4 (pg ***97***), **But the** _ _ _ _ *yeh-ho-**vaw*** [YHWH H3068 *n* the existing One, self-Existent Eternal] **sent out the great** _ _ _ _ .

What does that communicate, prove, or "speak" to you about God?

____

____

12❑ The shipmaster is responsible for all aboard the ship. Like those under his charge (the sailors), he fears for his life... ❍T ❍F ❍?

13❑ The shipmaster's concern shows he is: ❑ a Biblical **Believer** [trusting the truth of God's word by faith (that point of dependence upon God alone)] ❑ a **god-fearing** man [a person with a certain amount of respect for the higher deity; tries to live righteously, morally, but with limited understanding and devoid of the Holy Spirit] ❑ a **skeptic** [one who doubts the truth and reality of any principle or system of principles or doctrines; In theology, a person who doubts the existence and perfections of God] ❑ **superstitious** [belief in the direct agency of superior powers in certain extraordinary or singular events, or in omens (signs or indications of some supposed future event) and prognostics (foretelling; prediction)].

I can defend my answer based on: ❍ doctrine ❍ fact ❍ feeling ❍ guess ❍ hypothesis ❍ investigation ❍ judgment ❍ opinion ❍ Scripture ❍ theology ❍ theory (definitions pg ***61—62***). ☆ Worthy of discussion.
Scripture/address: ______________________________

14❑ The shipmaster believes ________________ controls the storm.

15❑ 1:5, who was afraid? ❍ Jonah ❍ the mariner's ❍ shipmaster

16❑ 1:6, who was afraid? ❍ Jonah ❍ the mariner's ❍ shipmaster

17❑ Who should be afraid? ❍ Jonah ❍ the mariner's ❍ shipmaster

18❑ The mariner's hope is **that we** _ _ _ _ _ _ [H6 v to be lost; lose oneself; to wander; to be destroyed; die; be exterminated; to be ready to perish, to be wretched, unfortunate; exterminated (judgment for sin); be ruined; vanish of memory, be forgotten; come to nothing]
_ _ _ [H3808 *conj* negation: opposed to affirmation; denial, refusal].

19❑ Did the mariners think they were going to die? .... ❍Y ❍N ❍?

20❑ Are mariners used to and familiar with storms at sea? ❍Y ❍N ❍?

21❑ Was their concern and reaction reasonable? .... ❍Y ❍N ❍?

Jonah 1:7 And they said every one to his fellow, Come, and let us cast lots, that we may know for whose cause this evil is upon us. So they cast lots, and the lot fell upon Jonah.

1❑ Handwrite Jonah 1:7. When a sentence is long, indent the next line as you continue. Remember to start on a new line after each punctuation mark (see page ***64***).

2❑ To whom does the phrase **"his fellow,"** [H7453 *n* associate; brother; companion; friend; neighbor] **refer to?**____________________

3❑ They got together and decided to _ _ _ _ [H5307 *n* to fall, by accident, chance] _ _ _ _ , [H1486 *n* rough, as stones, pebbles; figuratively, a portion or destiny as if determined by lot]

4❑ They sought to _ _ _ _ [H3045 *v* perceive; discern; know by experience; recognize; admit; acknowledge; confess] **something that wasn't obvious. What is your understanding or definition of "evil":**

◁ ◁ ◁ PAUSE Jonah 1:7

A❑ A form of the word **discern** [to separate by the eye, or by the understanding. Hence, to distinguish; to see or understand the difference between two or more things; to properly discriminate; to make a distinction; as, to discern between good and evil, truth and falsehood] occurs eighteen (18) times in the Bible. If possible, find each verse in your Bible, then read the entire chapter to get a better understanding of the context.

For each cross-reference listed, write the definition of discern you feel fits best, or your best understanding in your own words.

❍ *Genesis 31:32* (✍1450–1410 BC)

With whomsoever you find your gods, let him not live: before our brethren _ _ _ _ _ _ _ you what is yours with me, and take it to you. For Jacob knew not that Rachel had stolen them.

❍ *Genesis 38:25* (✍1450–1410 BC)

When she was brought forth, she sent to her father in law, saying, By the man, whose these are, am I with child: and she said, _ _ _ _ _ _ _ , I pray you, whose are these, the signet, and bracelets, and staff.

❍ *2 Samuel 14:17* (✍586–539 BC)

Then your handmaid said, The word of my lord the king shall now be comfortable: for as an angel of God, so is my lord the king to _ _ _ _ _ _ _ _ good and bad: therefore the Lord your God will be with you.

❍ *1 Kings 3:9–11* (✍586–539 BC)

9 **Give therefore your servant an understanding heart to judge**
your people, that I may _ _ _ _ _ _ _ _ between good and
bad: for who is able to judge this your so great a people? *10* **And**
the speech pleased the Lord, that Solomon had asked this thing.
11 **And God said to him, Because you have asked this thing, and**
have not asked for yourself long life; neither have asked riches
for yourself, nor have asked the life of your enemies; but have
asked for yourself understanding to _ _ _ _ _ _ _ judgment;

❍ *Ezra 3:13* (✍450 BC)

So that the people could not _ _ _ _ _ _ _ _ the noise of the shout of joy from the noise of the weeping of the people: for the people shouted with a loud shout, and the noise was heard afar off.

❍ *Job 4:16—17* (✍1450—1350 BC)

16 **It stood still, but I could not _ _ _ _ _ _ _ _ the form thereof: an image was before my eyes, there was silence, and I heard a voice, saying,** *17* **Shall mortal man be more just than God? shall a man be more pure than his maker?**

❍ *Ezekiel 44:23* (✍571 BC)

And they shall teach my people the difference between the holy and profane, and cause them to _ _ _ _ _ _ _ _ between the unclean and the clean.

❍ *Jonah 4:11* (✍785–760 BC)

And should not I spare Nineveh, that great city, wherein are more than sixscore thousand [120,000] **persons that cannot _ _ _ _ _ _ _ _ _ between their right hand and their left hand; and also much cattle?**

❍ *Malachi 3:18* (✍430 BC)

Then shall you return, and _ _ _ _ _ _ _ _ _ between the righteous and the wicked, between him that serves God and him that serves him not.

❍ *Matthew 16:3* (✍AD 60–65)

And in the morning, It will be foul weather to day: for the sky is red and lowering. O you hypocrites, you can _ _ _ _ _ _ _ _ _ the face of the sky; but can you not _ _ _ _ _ _ _ _ _ the signs of the times?

❍ *Luke 12:56* (✍AD 67–70)

You hypocrites, you can _ _ _ _ _ _ _ the face of the sky and of the earth; but how is it that you do not _ _ _ _ _ _ _ this time?

❍ *Hebrews 4:12* (✍AD 60–65)

For the word of God is quick, and powerful, and sharper than any twoedged sword, piercing even to the dividing asunder [separating] **of soul and spirit, and of the joints and marrow, and is a _ _ _ _ _ _ _ _ _ of the thoughts and intents of the heart.**

❍ *Hebrews 5:14* (✍AD 60–65)

But strong meat belongs to them that are of full age, even those who by reason of use have their senses exercised to _ _ _ _ _ _ _ both good and evil.

PERSEVERE Jonah 1:8

6❑ How could/would discernment help the sailors?

7❑ Read to understand the biblical definition of **evil** [H7451 n evil manner of thinking and acting; injurious, having qualities which tend to injury or produce mischief; what is displeasing to God and anyone; noxious (destructive), hurtful; sad of heart or mind; badness especially in an ethical sense; malignant; bad, unpleasant, giving pain, unhappiness, misery; vicious in disposition or temper; bad, evil, wicked of persons, thoughts, deeds, actions; corrupt; perverse; producing sorrow, distress, injury, calamity].

The word evil applies to some persons and behaviors. ..... ❍T ❍F ❍?
There are varying opinions of degrees of evil. .... ❍T ❍F ❍?
At times, the word evil could apply to me. .... ❍T ❍F ❍?
God is displeased with evil in any form. .... ❍T ❍F ❍?

8❑ Next, we'll go through the biblical definition of evil one by one to gain a more clear understanding that is easier to relate to:
Have you ever engaged in bad thinking/thoughts? .... ❍Y ❍N ❍?
... bad acting, actions, behavior, or deeds? .... ❍Y ❍N ❍?

9❑ Have you ever done something that injured or hurt another person (emotionally, physically, reputation, etc.)? .... ❍Y ❍N ❍?
... done something displeasing to God?............................. ❍Y ❍N ❍?
... something that made another sad in heart or mind?..... ❍Y ❍N ❍?
... something unethical (bad manners or morals)? .... ❍Y ❍N ❍?

10❑ Have you ever been the cause of pain to another? .... ❍Y ❍N ❍?

... the cause of unhappiness in another? .... ❍Y ❍N ❍?

... ever made another person's life miserable? .... ❍Y ❍N ❍?

... ever had corrupt conduct or that frame of mind? .... ❍Y ❍N ❍?

... ever acted out in anger or a bad temper? .... ❍Y ❍N ❍?

... ever produced distress, calamity, misery, misfortune? .. ❍Y ❍N ❍?

11❑ Have you ever felt *a slight degree or more of pleasure* from hurting someone, getting even, or from anything listed above?
❍Often ❍Once ❍Sometimes ❍Never ❍Sadly, Yes ❍Thankfully, No

12❑ The previous definition of evil is *not* **exhaustive** [includes all possibilities, is completely thorough and comprehensive; covers all or every important point].

Each of us is guilty of having participated in evil actions, attitudes, and behavior. We are all sinners (missing God's standards). There *are* levels of disobedience and evil. All are a transgression of God's law and an offense to Him.......................... ❍Agree ❍Disagree ❍?

13❑ Now that you have a better sense of the word evil, is it accurate to say Jonah had an evil manner of thinking and acting? ... ❍Y ❍N ❍?

Did Jonah's sin affect others? .... ❍Y ❍N ❍?

... produce **mischief** [harm; hurt; injury; damage; evil, whether intended or not; ill consequences], or **calamity** [great misfortune]? ...... ❍Y ❍N ❍?

... make anyone sad of heart or mind? .... ❍Y ❍N ❍?

... cause pain, unhappiness, or distress to others? .... ❍Y ❍N ❍?

Was Jonah's sin displeasing to God? .... ❍Y ❍N ❍?

14❑ The mariners believed the storm was "an act of God". ❍Y ❍N ❍?

15❑ They wanted to know **for whose cause** [H4310 *prep* who? what? which?] **this evil is upon us. So they** _ _ _ _   _ _ _ _

16❑ For each cross-reference listed, write of the purpose, result, additional knowledge or **insight** [sight or view of the inside or interior of anything (such as a problem or situation] you gain from the ancient practice of casting lots. Find each verse in your Bible, then read each chapter to better understand the context.

❍ *Leviticus 16:8* (✍1445—1444 BC)

And Aaron shall _ _ _ _ _ _ _ _ _ upon the two goats; one lot for the Lord, and the other lot for the scapegoat.

God directed ❍Y ❍N ❍? Mankind's idea ❍Y ❍N ❍?

❍ *Numbers 26:55—56* (✍1450—1410 BC)

55 **Notwithstanding the land shall be divided by _ _ _ _:**
according to the names of the tribes of their fathers they shall
inherit. *56* **According to the _ _ _ shall the possession thereof**
be divided between many and few.

God directed ❍Y ❍N ❍? Mankind's idea ❍Y ❍N ❍?

❍ *Joshua 18:6, 8, and 10* (✍1000—900 BC)

6 **You shall therefore describe the land into seven parts, and bring the description here** {hither} **to me, that I may _ _ _ _ _ _ _ _ for you here before the Lord our God.**

8 **And the men arose, and went away: and Joshua charged them that went to describe the land, saying, Go and walk through the**

land, and describe it, and come again to me, that I may here _ _ _ _ _ _ _ _ _ for you before the Lord in Shiloh.

10 **And Joshua _ _ _ _ _ _ _ _ _ for them in Shiloh before the Lord: and there Joshua divided the land to the children of Israel according to their divisions.**

God directed ❍Y ❍N ❍? Mankind's idea ❍Y ❍N ❍?

❍ *1 Samuel 14:42* (✍586–539 BC)

And Saul said, _ _ _ _ _ _ _ _ _ between me and Jonathan my son. And Jonathan was taken.

God directed ❍Y ❍N ❍? Mankind's idea ❍Y ❍N ❍?

❍ *1 Chronicles 24:31, 25:8, 26:13, 26:14* (✍430 BC)
The distribution of the duties of the priests and Levites offices.

❍ *Nehemiah 10:34, 11:1* (✍445–432 BC)
Revive and observe the duties neglected. Determine city dwellers.

❍ *Psalm 22:18* (✍1000–900 BC)

They part my garments among them, and _ _ _ _ _ _ _ _ _ upon my vesture [apparel, clothing, garment, raiment, vestment]**.**

God directed ❍Y ❍N ❍? Mankind's idea ❍Y ❍N ❍?

❍ *Proverbs 16:33* (✍1000–900 BC)

The _ _ _ is cast into the lap; but the whole disposing [act of deciding a case] **thereof is of the Lord.**

God directed ❍Y ❍N ❍? Mankind's idea ❍Y ❍N ❍?

❍ *Joel 3:3* (✍539–500 BC)
Israelite prisoners were counted of no value by their enemies.

❍ *Obadiah 1:11* (✍627–586 BC)
Foreigners looked upon Israel's affliction as sport.

❍ *Nahum 3:10* (✍663–612 BC)
Nineveh's once honored men now bound as prisoners, slaves.

❍ *Matthew 27:35* (✍AD 60–65)

And they crucified him, and parted his garments, _ _ _ _ _ _ _ _ _ _ _ _ _ : that it might be fulfilled which was spoken by the prophet, They parted my garments among them, and upon my vesture did they _ _ _ _ _ _ _ _ _ .

God directed ❍Y ❍N ❍? Mankind's idea ❍Y ❍N ❍?

❍ *Mark 15:24* (✍AD 55–65)

And when they had crucified him, they parted his garments, _ _ _ _ _ _ _ _ _ _ _ _ _ upon them, what every man should take.

God directed ❍Y ❍N ❍? Mankind's idea ❍Y ❍N ❍?

❍ *Luke 23:34* (✍AD 60)

Then said Jesus, Father, forgive them; for they know not what they do. And they parted his raiment, and _ _ _ _ _ _ _ _ _ .

God directed ❍Y ❍N ❍? Mankind's idea ❍Y ❍N ❍?

❍ *John 19:24* (✍AD 85–90)

They* (the heathen, pagan Roman soldiers) **said therefore among themselves, Let us not rend** [split, separate any substance into parts from end to end with force or sudden violence] **it, but _ _ _ _ _ _ _ _ _ for it, whose it shall be: that the scripture might be fulfilled, which says, They parted my raiment among them, and for my vesture they did _ _ _ _ _ _ _ _ _ . These things therefore the soldiers did.** *( ) Parenthesis added for clarity.*

God directed ❍Y ❍N ❍? Mankind's idea ❍Y ❍N ❍?

❍ *Acts 1:26* (✍AD 63–70)

And they gave forth their _ _ _ _ _ ; and the _ _ _ _ fell upon Matthias; and he was numbered with the eleven apostles.

God directed ❍Y ❍N ❍? Mankind's idea ❍Y ❍N ❍?

17❑ Describe what a "lot" is (see page ***133***):

18❑ I What is the general purpose or goal of casting lots?

19❑ In the English language, we use a few **idioms** [an expression peculiar from the common manner of speaking] such as: "flipping a coin, heads or tails" (to make a decision), "drawing the short straw" (to choose who will do an undesirable task), "rolling the dice" (hoping to win, have good luck, or take a chance in a risky decision).

Biblical "casting lots" is comparable to "flipping a coin." .. ❍T ❍F ❍?

...to "drawing the short straw" .... ❍T ❍F ❍?

...to "rolling the dice.".. ❍T ❍F ❍?

I use one of the above methods to determine
God's will and direction..........❍Always ❍Often ❍Sometimes ❍Never

20❍ What is your definition or understanding of gambling?

21❍ Betting, gambling, or the lottery is the same as casting lots. ....❍Agree ❍Disagree ❍?

22❍ Gambling etc., is harmless. .... ❍True ❍False ❍Not sure

23❍ How does the biblical practice of casting lots differ from betting, gambling (online or in person), participating in the lottery, etc.?

I can defend my answer based on: ❍ doctrine ❍ fact ❍ feeling ❍ guess ❍ hypothesis ❍ investigation ❍ judgment ❍ opinion ❍ Scripture ❍ theology ❍ theory (definitions pg ***61—62***). ☆ Worthy of discussion.
*Scripture/address:*________________

24❑ Jonah 1:8 And **the lot fell** [H5307 v to fall down, upon or from; cast or thrown down] **upon** _ _ _ _ _

25❑ In biblical times, it is believed the "lots" were controlled by:

NOTE: Do not confuse the man named Lot with a stick or stone "lot."

Jonah 1:8 Then said they to him, Tell us, we pray you for whose cause this evil is upon us; What is your occupation? and where come you? what is your country? and of what people are you?

1❑ Handwrite Jonah 1:8. When a sentence is long, indent the next line as you continue. Remember to start on a new line after each punctuation mark (see page ***64***).

2❑ Jonah is likely a stranger to everyone aboard ship...... ❍Y ❍N ❍?

3❑ Although the lot fell upon Jonah, the mariners still didn't know why. They **interrogate** [to examine by asking questions] Jonah face-to-face. Pay attention to the definitions that follow:

What is your _ _ _ _ _ _ _ _ _ _ [H4399 *n* deputyship, i.e., ministry, a special commission to act in the place of another; employment; work; business; industry; study; office; thing made; use; manner of work or workmanship]

4❑ **and** _ _ _ _ _ [H370 *conj* whence; from what place] **come you?**

5❑ **what is your _ _ _ _ _ _ _ _ ?** [H776 *n* land; country; territory; district; region; land of Canaan or Israel]

6❑ **and of what _ _ _ _ _ _ _** [H5971 *n* congregated unit; tribe; troop; flock; folk; men; nation] **are you ?**

7❑ We often mistakenly believe our sin does not affect others. But it does. Share a lesson learned from a sin committed that affected someone you know:

____

____

____

____

____

____

____

____

____

____

____

At the time, did you think you would "get away with it." .... ❍Y ❍N ❍?
... did you truly believe it wouldn't affect others? .... ❍Y ❍N ❍?
... did you even think of anyone but yourself .... ❍Y ❍N ❍?
... did it seem possible to flee from God's presence? .... ❍Y ❍N ❍?
... was someone suspicious of you or your behavior? .... ❍Y ❍N ❍?
... did someone try to "talk sense into you"?...................... ❍Y ❍N ❍?
... did someone confront you? .... ❍Y ❍N ❍?

Jonah 1:9 And he said to them, I am a Hebrew; and I fear the Lord, the God of heaven, which has made the sea and the dry land.

1❑ Handwrite Jonah 1:9 When a sentence is long, indent the next line as you continue. Remember to start on a new line after each punctuation mark (see page ***64***).

____

____

____

____

____

____

____

____

2❑ Jonah answers the mariner's last question. I am a _ _ _ _ _ _ [H5680 n ONE FROM BEYOND (a stranger or foreigner who immigrated into Canaan from beyond or the other side of the Euphrates river); Israelite is their sacred name, while Hebrew was for common use among non-Jews]

3❑ Write, in your own words, what the word **Hebrew** means:

____

____

____

Another name for a Hebrew is an Israelite.......................... ❍T ❍F ❍?

Another name for a Hebrew is a Jewish person (Jew)...... ❍T ❍F ❍?

Another name for a Hebrew is a Gentile (see page ***107***) ... ❍T ❍F ❍?

4❑ What does this first part of Jonah's answer reveal about him?

5❑ What does it mean to "**fear the Lord**"? *Guess if you don't know.*

6❑ If "I am a Hebrew" is Jonah 1:9a, what is Jonah 1:9b?

and ____

the ____

which ____

and ____

7❑ The word "Lord" [H3068] occurs 26 times in the book of Jonah and "God" [H430] occurs 16 times. How does the name/meaning of the **Lord** differ from the meaning of **God**?
Lord Yehôvâh *yeh-ho-**vaw*** [YHWH H3068 *n* the existing One, self-Existent Eternal]
God 'ĕlōhîm *el-o-**heem*** [H430 *n* specifically used of the Supreme God; the God of Abraham; God of gods; the true God; God of all flesh. It can also be used of a false god, heathen deity, or idol whom some worship in place of God]. Explain your understanding:

→

(continued): ______________________________

8❑ How can you determine when the use of God [H430] refers to the negative sense or use (i.e., a false god)?

9❑ What does Jonah acknowledge the Lord God has made:

the _ _ _ [H3220 *n* large body of water, specifically the Mediterranean Sea]

and [H853 *conj*] **the** _ _ _ _ _ _ _ [H3004 *n* that which is dry; dry ground as opposed to sea; specifically the shore of the sea at creation; figurative of needy Israel to be refreshed by God's spirit]**.**

10❑ Jonah states the Lord is **the God of** _ _ _ _ _ _ _ ,
[H8064 *n* firmament/expanse/region of air which surrounds the earth like an immense arch or vault; the higher ether: thin finer than air; where the celestial bodies revolve; the vast and infinite abode of God and angels]

11❑ There are multiple descriptions in the definition shown above. One is the _ _ _ that surrounds the earth, the next where _ _ _ _ _ _ _ _ _ _ _ _ [inhabitants of heaven] **bodies revolve, and additionally the** _ _ _ _ _ [place of continuance; dwelling; habitation] **of God and angels.**

12❑ Does Jonah believe God is the Creator................ ❍Yes ❍No ❍?

13❑ Does Jonah **fear the Lord**.................................... ❍Yes ❍No ❍?

Explain your answer:____

____

____

____

____

____

I can defend my answer based on: ❍ doctrine ❍ fact ❍ feeling ❍ guess ❍ hypothesis ❍ investigation ❍ judgment ❍ opinion ❍ Scripture ❍ theology ❍ theory (definitions pg ***61—62***). ☆ Worthy of discussion.

*Scripture/address:*____

14❑ Fear [H3373 *adj* morally reverent (submissive; humble; the highest degree of respect mingled with some degree of awe; a feeling or sentiment excited by the dignity and superiority of a person, or by the sacredness of his character); to be afraid; to stand in awe (fear mingled with admiration, reverence or a dread inspired by something great or terrific/terror) of; religious; pious (one who fears God); In scripture, fear is used to express a filial or a slavish (servant/submissive) passion. In good men, the fear of God is a holy awe or reverence of God and his laws, which springs from a just view and real love of the divine character, leading the subjects of it to hate and shun every thing that can offend such a holy being, and inclining them to aim at perfect obedience]

What does it mean to "**fear the Lord**"?

____

____

____

____

____

____

____

15❑ The ship's crew might be confused by Jonah's witness.. ❍Y ❍N ❍?

16❑ Is it possible to have a correct respect for God yet fail as a human to live or show it in your actions?............ ❍Y ❍N ❍?

Is *that* a good witness or testimony of a Believer?........... ❍Y ❍N ❍?

Have you ever failed to live according to your belief or faith? ❍Y ❍N ❍?

Is failure proof a person is not a genuine Believer?.......... ❍Y ❍N ❍?

Do you often hate and shun things that offend God......... ❍Y ❍N ❍?

Do you aim at, or for, obedience to God?.......................... ❍Y ❍N ❍?

Can you accurately state you **fear the Lord**?..................... ❍Y ❍N ❍?

Jonah 1:10 Then were the men exceedingly afraid, and said to him. Why have you done this? For the men knew that he fled from the presence of the Lord, because he had told them.

1❑ Handwrite Jonah 1:10. When a sentence is long, indent the next line as you continue. Remember to start on a new line after each punctuation mark (see page ***64***).

2❑ *Why* then were the men exceedingly _ _ _ _ _ _ _ , [H3372 v fear, be afraid; to stand in awe of; reverence (fear mingled with respect, esteem, and affection); honor: a painful emotion or passion excited by an expectation of evil, or the apprehension of impending danger]?

3❑ If you were there, would you have been afraid? .... ❍Y ❍N ❍?

Date: ____________

4❑ The men weren't just afraid, they were _ _ _ _ _ _ _ _ _ _ _ _ _ _ [H3373 *adj* going beyond, surpassing, excelling, outdoing, great in extent, quality, or duration; superabundant in magnitude and extent] **afraid.** How would you describe that level of fear in your own words?

5❑ Is there anything from your life story or experience that you can relate to being *exceedingly* afraid?................................ ❍Yes ❍No ❍?

6❑ The mariners are afraid of:................................... ❍ God ❍ Jonah

I can defend my answer based on: ❍ doctrine ❍ fact ❍ feeling ❍ guess ❍ hypothesis ❍ investigation ❍ judgment ❍ opinion ❍ Scripture ❍ theology ❍ theory (definitions pg **61–62**). ☆ Worthy of discussion.
Scripture/address:

7❑ Once again, the mariners interrogate. What did they ask Jonah?

1:10b **Why** [H4100 *part* what? how? why? when? what! how! for why? For what reason or cause] _ _ _ _ _ _ _ **done** [H6213 v to do, work, make, produce by labor; to manufacture, fabricate, fashion, create; to labor; to work about or upon anything; to prepare, attend to, put in order, appoint, ordain, institute; to bring about] **this** [H2063 *pron* this thing]**?**

❍ First, write 1:10b (above) without the definitions:

___

❍ Next, underline your opinion of the best definition (from above) to replace the word "done." You may have to change the verb ending to show the action correctly in the past, present, or future tense, i.e., worked in place of work, etc. Write your **paraphrased** [to explain, interpret, or translate a text to unfold the sense of the writing or attempt to add more clearness than is expressed in the words of the author and with latitude (room; space; openness, independence; freedom from confinement or restraint hence, looseness in exactness or precision)] sentence here:

___

___

❍ Underline the above word(s) you chose instead of "done".

Does it read well, flow smoothly, sound right?.................. ❍Y ❍N ❍?
Does it communicate the author's intent (in context)? ..... ❍Y ❍N ❍?
Is your text understandable—does it make sense? .... ❍Y ❍N ❍?

CAUTION: Although paraphrased Bibles can be easier to read and understand, the authenticity of God's word will be distorted and may mislead a reader. Paraphrased Bibles are often written by a sole author who decides which words and their meanings fit best according to that person's biases, beliefs, education, opinions, and understanding. Paraphrased text lacks the impact that God-breathed, carefully crafted words and sentences contain. On the positive side, paraphrased works can assist new Believers in beginning to read and understand the general teachings of the Bible. This study does not provide the Bible study tools necessary to accurately paraphrase a verse.

8❑ Jonah brought about trouble for the entire ship. ...**he had** _ _ _ _ [H5046 v to front, i.e., stand boldly out opposite; announce by word of mouth; expose; explain; declare; expound; profess; rehearse; show forth] **the mariners, that he fled from the presence of the Lord (or at least that's what he initially believed possible).**

9❑ Was Jonah **obligated** [*part* bound by contract or promise, or in a moral and legal sense; a duty which the law or good faith may enforce] to confess anything to anyone aboard ship? .... ❍Yes ❍No ❍?

I can defend my answer based on: ❍ doctrine ❍ fact ❍ feeling ❍ guess ❍ hypothesis ❍ investigation ❍ judgment ❍ opinion ❍ Scripture ❍ theology ❍ theory (definitions pg ***61—62***). ☆ Worthy of discussion.

Scripture/address: ____

10❑ Jonah **confessed** [to own, acknowledge or declare frankly and openly a crime, fault, charge, debt, or something that is against one's interest, or reputation; to declare to be true or to admit or assent to in words to disclose faults or the state of the conscience] the truth to strangers. That would be: ❍ easy ❍ difficult ❍ impossible (pg ***125***).

Have you (or someone you know) ever *"owned"* a mistake during the height of a **crisis** [a highly stressful point of time or the decisive state of things when a matter, state, or condition of concern reaches its highest tension and must soon be resolved, terminated, or suffer an impending change]? .... ❍Gladly ❍No ❍Reluctantly ❍Yes ❍?

Share: ____

____

____

____

____

☆ It would be nice to talk with someone about this subject.

◁ ◁ ◁ PAUSE Jonah 1:10

A❑ The word humble occurs twenty-five (25) times in the Bible with nine (9) different Strong's reference numbers and definitions. All of them are important to understand and apply to daily living. A sample verse is provided after each definition to give the sense of its use and meaning.

Mankind's natural, habitual, but too often **unconscious** [not knowing; not perceiving] tendency is: ❍ humility ❍ pride

English **antonyms** [opposites] to humble are egocentric, egotistical

a❍ **humble** [H3665 v to bend the knee, bow down, fall on one's knees; hence, to humiliate, vanquish (conquer, overcome, subdue in battle) self; bring down low into subjection or under, subdue self; to be depressed in spirit; to behave oneself submissively, especially before God]

❍ *2 Chronicles 7:14* (✍430 BC)

If my people, which are called by my name, shall _ _ _ _ _ _ themselves, and pray, and seek my face, and turn from their wicked ways; then will I hear from heaven, and will forgive their sin, and will heal their land.

b❍ **humble** [H6031 v to depress literally or figuratively; abase (lower, depress, cast down, reduce) self, afflict or chasten self; deal hardly with; bowed down; weaken; to exercise oneself in anything; to be afflicted, depressed, oppressed; submit oneself to anyone]

❍ *Deuteronomy 8:2* (✍1407–1406 BC)

And you shall remember all the way which the Lord your God led you these forty years in the wilderness, to _ _ _ _ _ _ you, and to prove you, to know what was in your heart, whether you would keep his commandments, or no.

c❍ humble [H6035 *n* from H6031: depressed (figuratively) in mind or circumstances; lowly, meek, poor, weak and afflicted; miserable, with the added notion of modest in mind (gentle) which prefers to bear injuries rather than return them]

❍ *Psalm 34:2* (✍1000–900 BC)

My soul shall make her boast in the LORD: the _ _ _ _ _ _ shall hear thereof, and be glad.

d❍ humble [H7807 *adj* sunk, downcast; low, lowly; depressed]

❍ *Job 22:29* (✍1450–1350 BC)

When men are cast down, then you shall say, There is lifting up; and he shall save the _ _ _ _ _ _ person.

e❍ humble [H7511 v to trample, i.e., to prostrate (lying in the posture of humility of adoration); tread; stamp oneself down; humble self, submit]

❍ *Proverbs 6:3* (✍1000–900 BC)

Do this now, my son, and deliver yourself, when you are come into the hand of your friend; go, _ _ _ _ _ _ _ yourself, and make sure your friend.

f❍ humble [H8213 v to depress or sink (especially figuratively, to humiliate; to bring, cast, or put down, debase (to reduce from a higher to a lower state or rank, in estimation), humble (self); to cast one's self down; be, bring, lay, make, put low or lower; to be lowly of spirit; set one in a lower place; metaphorically to be depressed or cast down from a high rank]

❍ *Jeremiah 13:18* (✍627–586 BC)

Say to the king and to the queen, _ _ _ _ _ _ _ yourselves, sit down: for your principalities shall come down, even the crown of your glory.

g❍ humble [H8217 *adj* depressed, literally or figuratively; low; humiliated; lowly]

❍ *Proverbs 16:19* (✍1000—900 BC)

Better it is to be of a _ _ _ _ _ _ _ spirit with the lowly, than to divide the spoil with the proud.

h❍ humble [*G5013* v to depress; figuratively, to humiliate in condition or heart; bring low, humble self; metaphorically, to bring into a humble condition, reduce to meaner (in want of dignity) circumstances; to assign a lower rank or place to; to be ranked below others who are honored or rewarded; one who submits to want; one who stoops to the condition of a servant; to lower, to depress one's soul, bring down one's pride; to have a modest opinion of oneself, to behave in an unassuming manner devoid of all haughtiness; to confess and deplore one's spiritual littleness and unworthiness]

❍ *1 Peter 5:6* (✍AD 64)

_ _ _ _ _ _ _ yourselves therefore under the mighty hand of God, that he may exalt you in due time:

i❍ humble [*G5011 adj* depressed, i.e., figuratively, humiliated in circumstances or disposition; cast down; of low degree or estate; lowly; not rising far from the ground]

James 4:6 (✍AD 44—46) **God resists the proud, but gives grace to the _ _ _ _ _ _ _.**

B❑ Briefly describe the meaning and actions of one who is **humble**:

____

____

____

____

C❑ Beginning at page ***163***, underline each definition of humble that **resembles** [to have the likeness of; to bear the similitude of something, either in form, figure or qualities; to liken; to compare; to represent as like something else] **your attitude** [a manner of behaving, feeling, or thinking which reflects your state of mind or disposition; a position of your body or the manner by which you carry yourself] **or behavior** [manner of behaving, whether good or bad; conduct; manners; carriage of one's self with respect to propriety (fitness; suitableness; appropriateness; agreement with established principles, rules or customs; justness; accuracy), or morals; deportment (manner of acting in relation to the duties of life; behavior; demeanor; conduct; management); external appearance or action] **consistently.**

D❑ Have you ever admitted something embarrassing, humiliating, etc., followed by choosing to "swallow your pride"............ ❍Y ❍N ❍?

Share more and/or the consequences of your decision:

____

____

____

____

____

____

☆ It would be nice to talk with someone about this subject.

E❑ Although the word "humble" is not in the Book of Jonah, the **concept** [thought; idea; principle] is. Turn back to page ***163*** again, circle every bullet point description of humble you feel Jonah **displayed** [to spread before the view; to show; to exhibit to the eyes or to the mind; to make manifest (plain, open, clearly visible to the eye or obvious to the understanding; apparent; not obscure or difficult to be seen or understood)].

PERSEVERE Jonah 1:10

11❑ Turn back to Jonah Chapter 1, page **7**, to review, in context, what happened in verses 1:5—10:

The mariners believed someone was the cause of evil, injurious, calamity displeasing to their god or God Supreme .... ❍T ❍F ❍?

They believed their god/God's will could be determined by casting lots ....❍Correct ❍Incorrect ❍?

They did *not* believe Jonah's attempt to flee from the presence of the Lord was the cause of the hurricane....... ❍T ❍F ❍?

12❑ This is what the mariners have done to understand and respond to the situation:

a) "... _ _ _ _ _ every man to his _ _ _ ..."

b) "... cast forth the _ _ _ _ _ that were in the ship into the _ _ _ ..."

c) Found _ _ _ _ _ asleep. Urged him to "... _ _ _ _ _ _ _ _ your God..."

d) "... cast _ _ _ _ to determine for _ _ _ _ _ cause this _ _ _ _ is upon us."

e) Confronted and interrogated _ _ _ _ _

f) Upon learning of Jonah's beliefs, they were "_ _ _ _ _ _ _ _ _ _ _ _ _ _ _ _ _ _ _, ..."

g) Confronted and interrogated again, asking "_ _ _ _ _ _ _ _ _ _ _ _ _ _ _ _ _ _ _ ?

13❑ What more could the mariners do beyond the actions reviewed. Or, what haven't they done that might make a difference or solve the problem? Think this through and consider ideas or ways you could have come up with a solution or action(s) you may have taken:

14❑ The mariners believe Jonah is the cause of the storm ❍T ❍F ❍?

15❑ I could believe Jonah is the cause of the storm .... ❍T ❍F ❍?

I can defend my answer based on: ❍ doctrine ❍ fact ❍ feeling ❍ guess ❍ hypothesis ❍ investigation ❍ judgment ❍ opinion ❍ Scripture ❍ theology ❍ theory (definitions pg ***61—62***). ☆ Worthy of discussion.

Scripture/address:

Jonah 1:11 Then said they to him, What shall we do to you that the sea may be calm to us? for the sea wrought, and was tempestuous.

1❏ Handwrite Jonah 1:11. When a sentence is long, indent the next line as you continue. Remember to start on a new line after each punctuation mark (see page ***64***).

____

____

____

____

____

____

____

____

2❏ The sailors confront Jonah with a question. Underline it above. Was this confrontation ❏ casual, or ❏ serious/strong?

Then _ _ _ _ **they** [H559 v uttered; expressed; commanded] **to him,** [H413 *prep* motion towards]

Would you guess it was: ❍ uttered, ❍ expressed, or ❍ commanded

3❏ Circle the word **you** in verse 1:11 above.

What [H4100 *part* what? how? why? when? what! how! for why?] **shall we** _ _ [H6213 v accomplish; advance; appoint; brought forth; fashioned; formed; created; produced] **to** _ _ _ [*prep*]

4❏ The mariners believe God has singled out Jonah as the problem that needs to be dealt with. ❍Yes ❍No ❍Uncertain

 Date: ____________

5❑ According to Jonah 1:4, the ship was like to be broken. In need of self-preservation, the mariners seek a **remedy** [that which counteracts an evil of any kind or repairs loss or disaster].

that the sea [H3220 *n* large body of water, specifically the Mediterranean Sea] **may be** _ _ _ _ [H8367 *v* subside; settle down; quiet; silent] **to** _ _ **?**

6❑ Is the mariners question **selfish** [regarding one's own interest chiefly or solely; influenced in actions by a view to private advantage; regard for self with disregard for others' well-being]? .... ❍Y ❍N ❍?

Why or why not:

I can defend my answer based on: ❍ doctrine ❍ fact ❍ feeling ❍ guess ❍ hypothesis ❍ investigation ❍ judgment ❍ opinion ❍ Scripture ❍ theology ❍ theory (definitions pg ***61–62***). ☆ Worthy of discussion.

Scripture/address: ______________________

7❑ I believe the storm is ❍ an "act of God" ❍ a coincidence ❍ a work of the devil ❍ mother nature ❍ unrelated.

8❑ The storm got the attention of ...... ❍ Jonah ❍ mariners ❍ others

9❑ for [H3588 *conj* yea indeed that; because, since; for though; but rather; so that, in order that; at that time; which; surely; forasmuch as] **the sea** [H3220 *n*] _ _ _ _ _ _ _ **,** [H1980 v was growing more and more stormy] **and was** _ _ _ _ _ _ _ _ _ _ _ [H5590 v raging; rushing; tossing; troubled; turbulent; rough with wind; blowing with violence]**.**

10❑ The storm situation has become more **desperate** [without hope; lost beyond hope of recovery; irretrievable; irrecoverable; great in the extreme]? **...........................** ❍Correct ❍Incorrect ❍I'm not sure

11❑ I have experienced feeling desperate.............. ❍True ❍False ❍?

☆ It would be nice to talk with someone about this subject.

Jonah 1:12 And he said to them, Take me up, and cast me forth into the sea; so shall the sea be calm to you: for I know that for my sake this great tempest is upon you.

1❑ Handwrite Jonah 1:12. When a sentence is long, indent the next line as you continue. Remember to start on a new line after each punctuation mark (see page ***64***).

____

____

____

____

____

____

____

____

2❑ Jonah answered the mariners, giving them directions on how to calm/settle down/quiet the sea. What are the sailors told to do:

1 _ _ _ _ _ _ _ _ _ , [H5375 v lift up; bear; carry; support; take away; carry off]

2 ...**and** _ _ _ _ _ _ _ _ _ _ _ _ [H2904 v to throw, cast, cast out] **into** [H413 *prep*] **the** _ _ _ ; [H3220 n large body of water, specifically the _ _ _ _ _ _ _ _ _ _ _ _ _ _ Sea]

3❑ Jonah's **remedy** [that which counteracts an evil of any kind, which cures uneasiness, or which repairs loss or disaster; reparation; to cure; to heal] **is odd** [extraordinary; differing from what is usual; strange; uncommon; in appearance not likely to answer the purpose] .. ❍Y ❍N ❍?

PAUSE Jonah 1:12

A❑ Which of the seven (7) continents are located around the Mediterranean Sea?

❍ Africa ❍ Antarctica ❍ Asia ❍ Australia
❍ Europe ❍ North America ❍ South America

NORTH AMERICA
EUROPE
ASIA
AFRICA
SOUTH AMERICA
AUSTRALIA
ANTARCTICA

B❑ Look at the map *on the next page*. Draw a ***circle*** around the **names** of the *European* countries located around the Mediterranean Sea (some are hard to locate and may be abbreviated). They are listed from left (Spain) clockwise to right (Greece).

❍ Spain ❍ France ❍ Monaco ❍ Italy ❍ Malta ❍ Slovenia ❍ Croatia
❍ Bosnia and Herzegovina ❍ Montenegro ❍ Albania ❍ Greece

C❑ Continuing around the map, draw a ***rectangle*** around the names of the *Asian* countries located around the Mediterranean Sea.

❍ Turkey ❍ Cyprus ❍ Syria ❍ Lebanon ❍ Israel

D❑ Now draw a triangle around the names of the *African* countries located around the Mediterranean Sea. They are listed from right (Egypt) to left (Morocco).

❍ Egypt ❍ Libya ❍ Tunisia ❍ Algeria ❍ Morocco

Biblical references to the Mediterranean include the Great Sea (Numbers 34, Joshua 1, 9, 15, 23, Ezekiel 47, 48), the Sea (1 Kings), and the Sea of the Philistines (Exodus 23:31). At one point in history, it is believed the Roman empire controlled all its coastline.

E❑ The number of countries located around the Mediterranean Sea:

European __________

Asian __________

African __________

Total* __________

*These countries are known today as the Mediterranean countries.

Random Whale Facts:

Whales have shown interest and positive responses to music, even swaying in appreciation. Search online for: "Mariachi Connecticut Serenades a Beluga Whale"

The blue whale's heart is a large as a smart car.

Some whale are born with albinism, a genetic condition which affects their pigmentation due to a lack of melanin in the skin or eyes. Albino (white or pale fur/skin) animals have difficulty camouflaging, which makes hiding from predators challenging.

Beluga whales are born with dark gray skin that turns naturally white over five to eight years of maturity.

When a whale slaps its tail on the water's surface it's a warning not to mess with it.

Narwhal males (and occasionally a female) have a tusk, up to 10 feet/3m long, protruding from its lip which is actually a spiral tooth. They are sometimes referred to as the "unicorn of the sea."

Blue whales look blue underwater but the top of the body is really a mottled gray.

Male humpback whales sing hitting almost every note on a piano. Their songs can last up to a half hour. Blue whales can sing up to 186 decibels, sperm whales reach 230 dB. Whale sound travels more than 1,000 miles.

Sperm whales sleep "standing up," vertically, in short 10-15 minute spurts between dinner and midnight.

The largest toothed predator on earth is the sperm whale.

Most whale are born tail-first to prevent drowning.

Whale fat is called blubber. Whales have 3 to 13 stomachs.

Adult male whale=bull, female whale=cow, baby whales=calves

PERSEVERE Jonah 1:12

4❏ What does **cast me forth** mean?

____

5❏ Underline your opinion of the best definition for each word/phrase below. Remember to keep the author's intention/purpose in context.

1:12 a **And he said** [H559 v to answer, bear forth, bring to light, declare; to say in the heart (think); to promise; command] **to them,** [H413 *prep* motion towards] **Take me up,** [H5375 v lift up; bear; carry; support; take away; carry off] **and cast me forth** [H2904 v to throw, cast, cast out] **into** [H413 *prep*] **the sea;** [H3220 *n* large body of water, specifically the Mediterranean Sea] **so shall the sea** [H3220 *n*] **be calm** [H8367 v subside; settle down; quiet; silent] **to you:** [H5921 *prep* on account or behalf of; among]

6❏ Paraphrase Jonah 1:12a. Choose either the original words/phrases, or your opinion of good replacement words/phrases that accurately define and explain the verse. The goal is to make the text easy to read and understand as though sharing with a child (see ***161***).

____

____

____

____

____

____

____

Does it read well, flow smoothly, and sound right?............ ❍Y ❍N ❍?
Does it communicate the author's intent (in context)? ..... ❍Y ❍N ❍?
Is your text understandable—does it make sense? .... ❍Y ❍N ❍?

7❑ Like the previous exercise, underline the parts of each definition that make Jonah's statement more understandable to you.

1:12b **for** [H3588 *conj* yea indeed that; because, since; for though; but rather; so that, in order that; at that time; which; surely; forasmuch as] **I** [H589 *pron* as for me] **know that** [H3045 v perceive; discern; know by experience; recognize; admit; acknowledge; confess] **for** [H3588 *conj*] **my sake** [H7945 *prep* on account of; because that] **this** [H2088 *pron* this one] **great** [H1419 *adj* going beyond, surpassing, excelling, outdoing, great in extent, quality, or duration; superabundant in magnitude and extent] **tempest** [H5591 *n* hurricane; storm; whirlwind; instrument of wrath; storm rushing with great velocity and extreme violence] **is** [H2088] this one here] **upon you** [H5921 *prep* super upon, when anything is put on the upper part of another so as to stand or lie upon it or have it for what is laid or spread under; used as a state of rest; on the basis/ground of; according to; on account or behalf of; concerning; beside; in addition to; together with; beyond; above; over; by; onto; towards; against]**.**

8❑ Paraphrase (see page *161*) Jonah 1:12b using words from the verse and any part of a definition [shown in brackets] **that helps you understand it better. Don't replace words if you feel the original states is best. Use as few words from a definition as possible.**

Does it read well, flow smoothly, and sound right?............ ❍Y ❍N ❍?
Does it communicate the author's intent (in context)? ..... ❍Y ❍N ❍?
Is your text understandable—does it make sense? .... ❍Y ❍N ❍?

9❑ Notice Jonah says I "know." Remembering he is a prophet of God, and has been spoken to by God previously, do you get the sense his statement is accurate, that God is communicating with him in a way Jonah can discern accurately?..................... ❍Y ❍N ❍?

10❑ Would/could God create a historic storm on account of one person?... ❍Yes ❍No ❍?

11❑ Innocent people can be affected when we sin ❍True ❍False ❍?

12❑ **Speculate** [meditate on; contemplate (view or consider with continued attention; study); consider a subject by turning it in the mind and viewing it in its different aspects and relations], why would/could God allow others to be affected by the sin of one person?

13❑ Here, Jonah exhibits: ❍ humility ❍ mental illness ❍ pride

14❑ Jonah selflessly considered others .... ❍Agree ❍Disagree ❍?

15❑ Jonah is suicidal......................... ❍Likely ❍Possibly ❍Unknown

16❑ Jonah knows how to swim .... ❍Likely ❍Possibly ❍Unknown

17❑ Imagine <u>you</u> are one of the sailors. You've experienced every part of the **chaos** [confusion; disorder], **danger** [risk; hazard; exposure to injury, loss, pain, or other evil], and **fear** [an expectation of evil or apprehension of impending danger] on board this vessel at sea. You, the master of the ship, and your **peers** [an equal; one of the same rank] have done everything you know to do, everything humanly possible. There are innocent people on board, passengers trusting in your abilities and experience as a professional on the open seas. Their lives are your responsibility. The ship is breaking apart, and nothing is left to lighten it. The leaders on board have prayed and trust the casting of lots was a reasonable way to get direction from their god. One person, the one the lot revealed, has admitted that because of him (Jonah), this great life-threatening hurricane of never-before-experienced violent wind is due to his decision to disobey his God. This person from a strange land, now wants you all to throw him overboard into the raging sea. He believes it will calm the angry wind and waves. If you don't do as he suggests, you believe everyone and everything will be lost at sea.

How **common** [usual; ordinary] is this situation in all of history?
With 10 being highest: ❍0 ❍1 ❍2 ❍3 ❍4 ❍5 ❍6 ❍7 ❍8 ❍9 ❍10

How **likely** [probable; that may be rationally thought or believed to have taken place in time past, or to be true now or hereafter; such as is more reasonable than the contrary] is it that Jonah is correct?
❍0 ❍1 ❍2 ❍3 ❍4 ❍5 ❍6 ❍7 ❍8 ❍9 ❍10

How likely is it for all leaders/persons on board to **agree** [be of one mind; harmonize in opinion]?
❍0 ❍1 ❍2 ❍3 ❍4 ❍5 ❍6 ❍7 ❍8 ❍9 ❍10

How likely is this situation to occur in today's modern times?
❍0 ❍1 ❍2 ❍3 ❍4 ❍5 ❍6 ❍7 ❍8 ❍9 ❍10

How likely is it you would disagree with Jonah?
❍0 ❍1 ❍2 ❍3 ❍4 ❍5 ❍6 ❍7 ❍8 ❍9 ❍10

Jonah 1:13 Nevertheless the men rowed hard to bring it to the land; but they could not: for the sea wrought, and was tempestuous against them.

1❑ Handwrite Jonah 1:13. When a sentence is long, indent the next line as you continue. Remember to start on a new line after each punctuation mark (see page ***64***).

2❑ Look back at page ***40***. Record dates for the Book of Jonah:

Possibly ✍ Written	*Possibly Occurred*
Jonah.............. _ _ _ BC	_ _ _ –_ _ _ BC

3❑ During the eighth century (799—700 BC), the construction of **sea-worthy** [fit for a voyage; worthy of being trusted to transport cargo with safety] ships varied widely and were powered by:
.... ❍electricity ❍engine/motor ❍rowing ❍sail ❍solar

4❑ In the eighth century, ships were:
......❍factory-made ❍hand-made ❍machine-made, ❍mass-produced

5❑ Rather than believe Jonah and throw him overboard, the mariners had one more idea. What did they do?

_ _ _ _ _ _ _ _ _ _ [H2864 v row (as digging into the water; to break through the waves)

to _ _ _ _ _ [H7725 v to cause to return; to turn back; come or go back; spiritually to turn back from or to God] **it to** [H413 *prep* motion toward] **the** _ _ _ _ ; [H3004 n dry ground]

6❑ They put heroic efforts of human strength into fighting the elements. How did that work out for them?

____

____

7❑ I have traveled on water by *human-powered* watercraft using:
...........❍oared craft ❍paddle craft ❍peddle craft ❍pole craft ❍other

8❑ I have experienced human-powered watercraft travel on a:

❍aqua-cycle ❍canoe ❍coracle ❍dinghy ❍dory ❍float/tube
❍hydrocycle ❍hydrofoil ❍kayak ❍kitesurf ❍makoro ❍punt
❍raft ❍row boat ❍sailboat ❍scull ❍skiff ❍skimboard
❍sup/paddleboard ❍surfboard ❍surfski ❍windfoil
❍windsail ❍windsup ❍windsurf ❍wingsurf

9❑ Circle the craft above you found difficult to: ❍learn, ❍master.

10❑ If you've ever rowed a boat, how easy is it to control?
With 10 being hardest: ❍0 ❍1 ❍2 ❍3 ❍4 ❍5 ❍6 ❍7 ❍8 ❍9 ❍10

11❑ The vessel Jonah boarded was:............❍one-level ❍multi-level

12❑ During a violent storm, rowing a vessel with cargo, mariners, and passengers would be:
....❍challenging ❍difficult ❍easy ❍impossible

13❑ The mariner's might be
.... ❍compassionate ❍control freaks ❍crazy

14❑ The mariners last-ditch effort seems:

❍ **Selfish** [regarding one's own interest chiefly or solely; influenced in actions by a view to private advantage] *(similar words/meanings: egotistical, inconsiderate, opportunistic, self-absorbed, self-centered, self-loving, self-obsessed, self-seeking, self-serving)*

❍ **Selfless** [having no concern for self] *(synonyms: altruistic, charitable, considerate, generous, self-denying, self-sacrificing, unselfish)*

❍ A combination of both.

Because:

____

____

____

____

____

____

____

____

____

____

I can defend my answer based on: ❍ doctrine ❍ fact ❍ feeling ❍ guess ❍ hypothesis ❍ investigation ❍ judgment ❍ opinion ❍ Scripture ❍ theology ❍ theory (definitions pg ***61—62***). ☆ Worthy of discussion.

*Scripture/address:*______________________________________

15❑ A mariner's job is ..❍challenging ❍difficult ❍easy ❍impossible

16❑ The sailors face increasingly bad weather on the Mediterranean Sea (which is huge). It occupies an area of just under one million square miles/2,589,988 km. You can fit four states of Texas or a quarter of the United States within it.

the sea [H3220 *n* large body of water, specifically the Mediterranean Sea] _ _ _ _ _ _ _ _ [H1980 v was growing more and more stormy]**, and was** _ _ _ _ _ _ _ _ _ _ _ _ [H5590 v raging; rushing; tossing; troubled; turbulent; rough with wind; blowing with violence] **against them** [H5921 *prep*]

17❑ Tempestuous weather could cause even the most seasoned sailor to suffer sea sickness. If you were on board, which descriptions of the definition are most likely to affect you (choose two or more):

❍ **Raging** [acting with violence or fury; vehemently driven or agitated]
❍ **Rushing** [a violent driving of anything; rapid or tumultuous course]
❍ **Tossing** [throwing upward; rising, falling, rolling, tumbling suddenly]
❍ **Troubled** [disturbed; agitated; afflicted; annoyed]
❍ **Turbulent** [disturbed; tumultuous; restless; disordered commotion]
❍ **Rough** [inequal; thrown into huge waves; violent, severe; dreadful]
❍ **Violent** [driven with force; vehement; outrageous; fierce; extreme]

18❑ Although sea sickness *(aka motion sickness)* won't kill you, the complications of dehydration, low blood pressure, nausea, sweating, vomiting, plus reduced abilities, and mobility compound risks and recovery. It can take days to feel back to normal once you are removed from the cause. **Sea sickness** [affected with sickness or nausea from the pitching or rolling of a vessel] is a miserable experience.

If you've ever been sea sick, how would you rate the feeling?
10=you're "dying": ❍0 ❍1 ❍2 ❍3 ❍4 ❍5 ❍6 ❍7 ❍8 ❍9 ❍10

19❑ Is it possible one or all mariners were sea-sick .... ❍T ❍F ❍?

20❑ Is it possible Jonah was sea-sick................................ ❍T ❍F ❍?

21❑ It is likely I would be sea-sick ....❍Correct ❍Incorrect ❍?

Jonah 1:14 Wherefore they cried to the Lord, and said, We beseech you O Lord, we beseech you let us not perish for this man's life, and lay not upon us innocent blood: for you, O Lord, have done as it pleased you.

1❏ Handwrite Jonah 1:14. When a sentence is long, indent the next line as you continue. Remember to start on a new line after each punctuation mark (see page ***64***).

2❏ The mariner's cry and prayer is:

We _ _ _ _ _ _ _ _ **you** [H577 *part* an interjection of entreaty: Ah, I pray! oh, now!; pray now!] **O Lord** [H3068 *n*], **we** _ _ _ _ _ _ _ _ **you** [H4994 *part* as an exhortation: oh may it be] **let us not perish for this man's life,...**

Two distinct Hebrew words for beseech are simplified in English as one. The first is an interjection, which strengthens the emotion of the request. The second use is demonstrative to direct the attention of the listener.

This prayer is used to:

❍encourage ❍express emotion ❍persuade ❍urge

3❑ Previously, the mariners cried for help:

1:5 **Then the mariners were afraid, and cried** [H2199 v to cry out; to proclaim; to call upon; call together; assemble] **every man to his god,** 'ĕlōhîm *el-o-**heem*** [H430 *n* used poetically, gods in the ordinary sense; can apply to a false god, heathen deity, or idol]

Here, they cry for help again:

1:14 **Wherefore they cried** [H7121 v utter a loud sound; cry for help; address by name; call out to] **to** [H413 *prep* motion towards] **the Lord,** [Yehôvâh *yeh-ho-**vaw*** [YHWH H3068 *n* the existing One, self-Existent Eternal]

What is different between the two **pleas** [urgent prayer, entreaty (petition; pressing solicitation)]?

____

____

____

____

____

____

4❑ The sailor's first request is:

1:14b ...**let us not** [H408 *part* nothing; nay; never; no] _ _ _ _ _ _ [H6 v to be lost; lose oneself; to wander; to be destroyed; die; be exterminated; to be ready to perish, to be wretched, unfortunate; exterminated (judgment for sin); be ruined; vanish of memory, be forgotten; come to nothing] **for** _ _ _ _ [H2088 *pron* this one] **man's** [H376 *n* male or husband (in contrast to female or wife); human being (in contrast to God); mankind; one another; anyone; someone; person] _ _ _ _ **,** [H5315 *n* soul; breathing creature (distinguished from body), i.e., animal of vitality; a living breathing being whose life resides in the blood; the seat of appetite, desire, emotion, passion]...

5❑ So far, Jonah's **testimony** [open affirmation, attestation, or declaration made for the purpose of establishing or proving some fact] **or witness** [a testimony of a person who knows or sees anything; that which furnishes evidence or proof] **is:**

❍ **bad** [corrupt; defective; depraved; evil; hurtful].
❍ **contradictory** [inconsistent; opposite; a denial of what has been asserted; moving against or in the opposite direction].
❍ **good** [valid; having strength adequate to its support; not defective; complete or sufficiently perfect in its kind; having the physical qualities best adapted to its design and use; sound; not weak, false or fallacious; uncorrupted; undamaged; full; complete; useful; valuable; honorable; fair; unblemished; kind; friendly; humane].
❍ **hypocritical** [a false appearance of what is good; concealing one's real character or motives; feigning what he is not; one who has the form of godliness without the power, or who assumes an appearance of piety and virtue (moral goodness), when he is destitute of true religion; without sincerity].

Because:

____

____

____

____

____

____

____

I can defend my answer based on: ❍ doctrine ❍ fact ❍ feeling ❍ guess ❍ hypothesis ❍ investigation ❍ judgment ❍ opinion ❍ Scripture ❍ theology ❍ theory (definitions pg ***61–62***). ☆ Worthy of discussion.

Scripture/address: ______________________________

6❑ The Bible teaches the general truth of being careful with whom you **associate** [to join in company, as a friend, companion; unite in action; join in interest or purpose]. In the following cross-references, circle the things or persons you should avoid. *NOTE: Definitions added for clarity.*

❍ *Psalm 1:1–2* (✍499–400 BC)

1 **Blessed is the man that walks not in the counsel of the ungodly, nor stands in the way of sinners, nor sits in the seat of the scornful.** 2 **But his delight is in the law of the Lord; and in his law does he meditate day and night.**

❍ *Psalms 26:5* (✍1000–900 BC)

I have hated the congregation of evil doers; and will not sit with the wicked.

❍ *Proverbs 13:20* (✍1000–900 BC)

He that walks with wise men shall be wise: but a companion of fools shall be destroyed.

❍ *Proverbs 14:7* (✍1000–900 BC)

Go from the presence of a foolish man, when you perceive not in him the lips of knowledge.

❍ *1 Corinthians 5:11* (✍AD 55–56)

But now I have written to you not to keep company, [mix up together with; associate or be intimate with] **if any man that is called a brother be a fornicator, or covetous, or an idolater, or a railer** [abusive]**, or a drunkard, or an extortioner; with such a one no not to eat.**

❍ *1 Corinthians 15:33* (✍AD 55–56)

Be not deceived: evil communications [companionship; intercourse; communion] **corrupt good manners.** [morals; habits; character]

❍ *2 Corinthians 6:14* (✍AD 56—57)

Be you not unequally yoked [have fellowship with one who is not an equal, i.e., Believer's with idolaters; the union of beasts of different kinds, e. g. an ox and an ass] **together with unbelievers:** [those without trust and faith in Christ] **for what fellowship** [participation; sharing; communion] **has righteousness with unrighteousness? and what communion has light with darkness?**

7❑ Jonah was a paying passenger, and the sailors were paid employees. There is no evidence of an overly familiar or close association between the parties. Naturally, no one on board the ship wanted to die for the life/soul of another. What is the sailors' second request?

1:14c ...**and lay not upon us** _ _ _ _ _ _ _ _ _ _ [H5355 *adj* blameless; clean; free from punishment; exempt of obligation; guiltless]
blood: [H1818 *n* as that which when shed causes death; bloodshed, slaughter and the guilt contracted by killing] ...

8❑ What are they asking of the Lord?

____

____

____

____

____

9❑ What would you ask of the Lord if you were "in their shoes?"

____

____

____

____

10❑ Although God is love (1 John 4:8), he **hates** [as an enemy, foe, adversary; a great dislike or aversion (opposition or repugnance of mind); has no affection for] **sin and wickedness such as idolatry, ungodly sacrifices, sexual perversion, evildoers, and more. The list below mentions some (not all) sins we would do well to avoid. Left unchecked, our thoughts can progress to wicked deeds, so beware.**

❍ *Proverbs 6:16—19* (✍1000—900 BC)

16 These six things does the Lord hate: yea, seven are an abomination [wickedness; something disgusting (morally), i.e., an abhorrence; something made impure and illicit (not permitted or allowed; prohibited; unlawful)] **to him: 17 A proud look, a lying tongue, and hands that shed innocent blood, 18 A heart that devises wicked imaginations, feet that be swift in running to mischief, 19 A false witness that speaks lies, and he that sows discord among brethren.**

11❑ The cross-reference above was **penned** [written] ❍ before ❍ after the time of Jonah.

12❑ *Briefly* state *(in your own words)* the seven hated things listed.

1 ______________________________

2 ______________________________

3 ______________________________

4 ______________________________

5 ______________________________

6 ______________________________

7 ______________________________

❍ Circle the ones that can be traced to originating from our heart.

13❑ The sailor's prayer requested two things:

1) **...let _ _ not perish for this man's life...** *and*

2) **...lay not upon _ _ innocent blood...**

14❑ What do you notice about the Lord/God from this Psalm?

❍ *Psalm 135:5-7* (✍499—400 BC)

5 For I know that the Lord is great, and that our Lord is above all gods. 6 Whatsoever the Lord pleased, that did he in heaven, and in earth, in the seas, and all deep places. 7 He causes the vapors to ascend from the ends of the earth; he makes lightnings for the rain; he brings the wind out of his treasuries.

15❑ And, the sailors reasoning?

_ _ _ [H3588 *conj* yea indeed that; because, since; for though; but rather; so that, in order that; at that time; which; surely; forasmuch as] **you** [H859 *pron*]**, O Lord** [H3068 *n*]**, have done** [H6213 v to do, work, make, produce by labor; to manufacture, fabricate, fashion, create; to labor; to work about or upon anything; to prepare, attend to, put in order, appoint, ordain, institute; to bring about] **as it** [H834 *prep* on account of whom? that, since, as; condition if] _ _ _ _ _ _ _ _ _ _ [H2654 v to delight or take pleasure in].

Jonah 1:15 So they took up Jonah, and cast him forth into the sea: and the sea ceased from her raging.

1❑ Handwrite Jonah 1:15. When a sentence is long, indent the next line as you continue. Remember to start on a new line after each punctuation mark (see page ***64***).

2❑ With all options exhausted, the sailors face an unimaginable task. Lift up/bear/carry/support/take away/carry off Jonah, a living, breathing human being. And, throw him overboard!

Would any sound-minded person want to accept responsibility for that act? .... ❍Y ❍N ❍?

3❑ Did the mariners believe Jonah? .... ❍Y ❍N ❍?

My guess is they responded out of: ❍ belief ❍ faith ❍ hatred ❍ hope ❍ lack of empathy ❍ racial discrimination ❍ revenge ❍ other:

4❑ Did the men trust the *Lord* was doing as *He* pleased?. ❍Y ❍N ❍?

5❑ Is there any indication Jonah resisted? .... ❍Y ❍N ❍?

6❑ Do the sailors seem to be of a sound mind? .... ❍Y ❍N ❍?

Does Jonah seem **sane** [having the regular exercise of reason and other faculties of the mind; healthy; not disordered or shattered]?..... ❍Y ❍N ❍?

7❑ Does anyone seem **crazy** [broken; decrepit; feeble; weak or disordered in intellect or shattered in mind; deranged]? .... ❍Y ❍N ❍?

 Date: ____________

8❑ Turn to page ***175*** to review 1:12. What did Jonah tell the sailors?

A) T __________________________________

B) C __________________________________

... and the result would be:

____

9❑ Now Jonah states: 1:12b **for** _ _ _ _ _ _ [H3045 v perceive; discern; know by experience; recognize; admit; acknowledge; confess] **for** _ _ **sake** [H7945 *prep* on account of; because that] **this great tempest is upon you.**

10❑ It appears Jonah was ❍ confident ❍ convinced ❍ confused ❍ crazy

11❑ Jonah had discernment (page ***134***) from the Lord ..... ❍T ❍F ❍?

12❑ 1:15 **So they** _ _ _ _ _ _ _ [H5375 v lift up; bear; carry; support; take away; carry off] **Jonah,** *yoh-**naw*** [H3124 *n* DOVE; a gentle term of endearment; weak, gentle, feeble] **and cast him forth** [H2904 v to throw, cast, cast out] **into** [H413 *prep* motion towards] **the sea:** [H3220 *n* large body of water, specifically the Mediterranean Sea]...

13❑ The sailors pushed Jonah off the boat... ❍Agree ❍Disagree ❍?

... **and the sea** [H3220 *n*] _ _ _ _ _ _ _ _ [H5975 v stand still; stop moving or doing] **from her** _ _ _ _ _ _ _ _ [H2197 v storming; indignation; anger].

14❑ Jonah was/is a prophet of the Lord God .... ❍True ❍False ❍?

15❑ How long did it take for the sea to calm?

____

16❑ The prophecy, through Jonah, came true. .... ❍T ❍F ❍?

17❑ Jonah "heard" from the Lord accurately .... ❍T ❍F ❍?

18❑ A true prophet is: (choose ones that apply)

❍ One who speaks or sings by **inspiration** [the infusion of ideas into the mind by the Holy Spirit; the conveying into the minds of men, ideas, notices or monitions by extraordinary or supernatural influence; or the communication of the divine will to the understanding by suggestions or impressions on the mind, which leave no room to doubt the reality of their supernatural origin] in **prediction** [to tell beforehand something that is to happen].

❍ One who sings or speaks by inspiration in a speech or **sermon** [a discourse delivered in public by licensed clergymen for religious instruction, and usually grounded on some text or passage of Scripture].

❍ One who pours forth words abundantly with **divine** [pertaining to the true God] affection, emotion of mind, and passion.

❍ One who **foretells** [to predict; to tell before an event happens; to prophesy] future events, a foreteller, predictor.

❍ One who is **illuminated** [to enlighten; to throw light on; to supply with light; to enlighten intellectually with knowledge or grace; to illustrate; to throw light on, as on obscure subjects] inspired or instructed by God to announce future events.

❍ One who explains or communicates **sentiments** [a thought prompted by passion or feeling; thought; opinion; notion; judgment; the decision of the mind formed by deliberation or reasoning].

❍ A foreteller, by **analogy,** [an agreement or likeness between things in some circumstances or effects, when the things are otherwise entirely different, i.e., Learning enlightens the mind, because it is to the mind, what light is to the eye, enabling it to discover things before hidden] an inspired speaker.

19❑ It is likely the sailors have a high degree of respect (mingled with awe) of the dignity and superiority of the Lord God. .. ❍T ❍F ❍?

PAUSE Jonah 1:15

A❑ FYI, all of the definitions on the previous page correctly describe a true prophet of God. Describe/define the meaning of the word: **True**

B❑ Describe/define the meaning of the word: **False**

C❑ What then is a false prophet?

D❑ Who do false prophets claim to represent?

E❑ The Bible reveals the characteristics of true prophets of God (those who represent Him accurately) in contrast to false fakers.

The Lord expects His people to determine the true from false. Believers are tasked with paying attention to what people say ***and*** what they do. It's not someone else's responsibility—*it's ours!*

Read the following cross-references to recognize the characteristics of true versus false prophets. Once you understand the passages, mark the bubble TP if the instruction or warning is for or about a True Prophet and FP for False (unless the verse(s) addresses both).

❍ *Deuteronomy 18:18—22* (✍1407—1406 BC) ❍ *TP* ❍ *FP* ❍ *Both*

18 **I will raise them up a Prophet** [inspired man] **from among their brethren, like to you, and will put my words in his mouth; and he shall speak to them all that I shall command him.** *19* **And it shall come to pass, that whosoever will not hearken** [hear; listen; obey] **to my words which he shall speak in my name, I will require it of him.** *20* **But the prophet, which shall presume to speak a word in my name, which I have not commanded him to speak, or that shall speak in the name of other gods, even that prophet shall die.** *21* **And if you say in your heart, How shall we know the word which the Lord has not spoken?** *22* **When a prophet speaks in the name of the Lord, if the thing follow not, nor come to pass, that is the thing which the Lord has not spoken, but the prophet has spoken it presumptuously: you shall not be afraid of him.**

❍ Underline the words and verses by which you are impacted, touched, or impressed. Use the blank lines to note questions, thoughts, or anything else you want to share or research.

____

____

____

❍ *Jeremiah 14:14* (✍627—586 BC) ❍ *TP* ❍ *FP* ❍ *Both*

Then the LORD said to me, The prophets prophesy lies in my name: I sent them not, neither have I commanded them, neither spoke to them: they prophesy to you a false vision and divination, [witchcraft] **and a thing of nought,** [no value; worthless] **and the deceit of their heart.**

❍ *Jeremiah 23:21-40* (✍627—586 BC) ❍ *TP* ❍ *FP* ❍ *Both*

21 **I have not sent these prophets, yet they ran: I have not spoken**
to them, yet they prophesied. *22* **But if they had stood in my**
counsel, and had caused my people to hear my words, then they
should have turned them from their evil way, and from the evil of
their doings. *23* **Am I a God at hand, says the Lord, and not a God**
afar off? *24* **Can any hide himself in secret places that I shall not**
see him? says the Lord. Do not I fill heaven and earth? says the
Lord. *25* **I have heard what the prophets said, that prophesy lies**
in my name, saying, I have dreamed, I have dreamed. *26* **How**
long shall this be in the heart of the prophets that prophesy lies?
yea, they are prophets of the deceit of their own heart; *27* **Which**
think to cause my people to forget my name by their dreams
which they tell every man to his neighbor, as their fathers have
forgotten my name for Baal. [a Phoenician deity/god] *28* **The prophet**
that has a dream, let him tell a dream; and he that has my word,
let him speak my word faithfully. What is the chaff to the wheat?
says the Lord. *29* **Is not my word like as a fire? says the Lord; and**
like a hammer that breaks the rock in pieces? *30* **Therefore,**

behold, I am against the prophets, says the Lord, that steal my
words every one from his neighbor. *31* Behold, I am against the
prophets, says the Lord, that use their tongues, and say, He says.
32 Behold, I am against them that prophesy false dreams, says
the Lord, and do tell them, and cause my people to err by their
lies, and by their lightness; yet I sent them not, nor commanded
them: therefore they shall not profit this people at all, says the
Lord. *33* And when this people, or the prophet, or a priest, shall
ask you, saying, What is the burden of the Lord? you shall then
say to them, What burden? I will even forsake you, says the Lord.
34 And as for the prophet, and the priest, and the people, that
shall say, The burden of the Lord, I will even punish that man and
his house. *35* Thus shall you say every one to his neighbor, and
every one to his brother, What has the Lord answered? and, What
has the Lord spoken? *36* And the burden of the Lord shall you
mention no more: for every man's word shall be his burden; for
you have perverted the words of the living God, of the Lord of
hosts our God. *37* Thus shall you say to the prophet, What has
the Lord answered you? and, What has the Lord spoken? *38* But
since you say, The burden of the Lord; therefore thus says the
Lord; Because you say this word, The burden of the Lord, and I
have sent to you, saying, You shall not say, The burden of the
Lord; *39* Therefore, behold, I, even I, will utterly forget you, and I
will forsake you, and the city that I gave you and your fathers,
and cast you out of my presence: *40* And I will bring an everlasting
reproach upon you, and a perpetual shame, which shall not
be forgotten.

❍ *Jeremiah 29:8-9* (✍627—586 BC) ❍ *TP* ❍ *FP* ❍ *Both*

8 **For thus says the Lord of hosts, the God of Israel; Let not your prophets and your diviners,** [one who practices divination, foretelling future events, or discovering things secret or obscure, by the aid of superior beings, or by other than human means; done or said by guess; to presage (to indicate by some present fact what is to follow or come to pass); prediction; soothsayer (a foreteller; one who undertakes to foretell future events by present signs, without inspiration); necromancer (one who pretends to foretell future events by holding converse with departed spirits; a conjurer, one who pretends to the secret art of performing things supernatural or extraordinary, by the aid of superior powers; an impostor who pretends, by unknown means, to discover things); to call forth of the dead; one who pretends to predict events, or to reveal occult things, by the aid of superior beings, or of supernatural means; a conjecturer (one who guesses; a guesser; one who forms or utters an opinion without proof)] **that be in the midst of you, deceive you, neither hearken to your dreams which you cause to be dreamed.** *9* **For they prophesy falsely to you in my name: I have not sent them, says the Lord.**

❍ *Ezekiel 13:1-8* (✍571 BC) ❍ *TP* ❍ *FP* ❍ *Both*

1 **And the word of the Lord came to me, saying,** *2* **Son of man, prophesy against the prophets of Israel that prophesy, and say you to them that prophesy out of their own hearts, Hear you the word of the Lord;** *3* **Thus says the Lord God; Woe to the foolish**

prophets, that follow their own spirit, and have seen nothing!
4 **O Israel, your prophets are like the foxes in the deserts.** *5* **You**
have not gone up into the gaps, neither made up the hedge for
the house of Israel to stand in the battle in the day of the Lord.
6 **They have seen vanity and lying divination, saying, The Lord**
says: and the Lord has not sent them: and they have made others
to hope that they would confirm the word. *7* **Have you not seen a**
vain vision, and have you not spoken a lying divination, whereas
you say, The Lord says it; albeit I have not spoken? *8* **Therefore**
thus says the Lord God; Because you have spoken vanity,
[uselessness; emptiness; nothingness] **and seen lies, therefore,**
behold, I am against you, says the Lord God.

❍ *Zechariah 10:2* (✍480 BC) ❍ *TP* ❍ *FP* ❍ *Both*

For the idols have spoken vanity, [panting in vain; to come to nothingness] **and the diviners** [magicians; soothsayers] **have seen a lie, and have told false dreams; they comfort in vain: therefore they went their way as a flock, they were troubled, because there was no shepherd.**

❍ *Matthew 7:15-23* (✍AD 15—23) ❍ *TP* ❍ *FP* ❍ *Both*

15 **Beware of false prophets, which come to you in sheep's**
clothing, but inwardly they are ravening wolves. *16* **You shall**
know them by their fruits. Do men gather grapes of thorns, or
figs of thistles? *17* **Even so every good tree brings forth good**
fruit; but a corrupt tree brings forth evil fruit. *18* **A good tree**
cannot bring forth evil fruit, neither can a corrupt tree bring forth
good fruit. *19* **Every tree that brings not forth good fruit is hewn**
down, and cast into the fire. *20* **Wherefore by their fruits you**
shall know them. *21* **Not every one that says to me, Lord, Lord,**
shall enter into the kingdom of heaven; but he that does the will
of my Father which is in heaven. *22* **Many will say to me in that**
day, Lord, Lord, have we not prophesied in your name? and in
your name have cast out devils? and in your name done many
wonderful works? *23* **And then will I profess to them, I never**
knew you: depart from me, you that work iniquity [illegality; violation
or transgression of the law; wickedness; unrighteousness]**.**

❍ *Matthew 24:4-13* (✍AD 60—65) ❍ *TP* ❍ *FP* ❍ *Both*

4 **And Jesus answered and said to them, Take heed that no man**
deceive you. *5* **For many shall come in my name, saying, I am**
Christ; and shall deceive many. *6* **And you shall hear of wars and**
rumors of wars: see that you be not troubled: for all these things
must come to pass, but the end is not yet. *7* **For nation shall rise**
against nation, and kingdom against kingdom: and there shall
be famines, and pestilences, and earthquakes, in divers [various]

places. *8* **All these are the beginning of sorrows.** *9* **Then shall
they deliver you up to be afflicted, and shall kill you: and you
shall be hated of all nations for my name's sake.** *10* **And then
shall many be offended, and shall betray one another, and shall
hate one another.** *11* **And many false prophets shall rise, and
shall deceive many.** *12* **And because iniquity shall abound, the
love of many shall wax cold.** *13* **But he that shall endure to the
end, the same shall be saved.**

❍ *Mark 13:21–22* (✍AD 55–65) ❍ *TP* ❍ *FP* ❍ *Both*

21 **And then if any man shall say to you, Lo, here is Christ;** [anointed, the Messiah, and epithet of Jesus Christ; the Christ Messiah who is Jesus; the person of Christ, who by His holy power and Spirit lives in the souls of His followers, and so molds their characters that they bear His likeness] **or, lo, he is there; believe him not:** *22* **For false Christs** [a spurious (not genuine; not proceeding from the true source, or from the source pretended; counterfeit; false; adulterate; not legitimate) Messiah; one who falsely lays claim to the name and office of the Messiah] **and false prophets shall rise, and shall show signs and wonders, to seduce,** [cause to go astray (go out of the right way or proper place, both in a literal and figurative sense); to lead away from the truth to error; stray away from] **if it were possible, even the elect** [the picked out; those who choose salvation through Christ; chosen by God]**.**

❍2 *Peter 2:1* (✍AD 64–65) ❍ *TP* ❍ *FP* ❍ *Both*

But there were false prophets also among the people, even as there shall be false teachers [propagators of erroneous Christian doctrine] **among you, who privily shall bring in** [secretly or craftily] **damnable** [destroying, destructive] **heresies,** [disunion; one's chosen opinion varying from the true exposition of the Christian faith] **even denying the Lord that bought them, and bring upon themselves swift destruction.**

❍ *1 John 4:1* (✍AD 80–85) ❍ *TP* ❍ *FP* ❍ *Both*

Beloved, believe not every spirit, but try the spirits [an immaterial (not consisting of matter, imponderable such as electricity) intelligent (has the faculty of understanding or reason) substance possessing the power of acting, deciding, desiring, doubting, knowing, moving, thinking, etc.) Hence, an immaterial intelligent being] **whether they are of God: because many false prophets are gone out into the world.**

The Bible reveals much about the behavior of false prophets for our learning. Keep alert!

F❑ If someone quotes the Bible, "chapter and verse," it's proof they represent God accurately ...... ❍Yes ❍Maybe ❍No ❍Not necessarily

G❑ If someone opposed to God quotes the Bible, it will probably be a quote taken out of context .... ❍Agree ❍Disagree ❍?

H❑ Can false prophets speak on behalf of false gods? .... ❍Y ❍N ❍?

I❑ Is deception a characteristic of false prophets? .... ❍Y ❍N ❍?

J❑ Might false prophets be associated with witchcraft? .. ❍Y ❍N ❍?

K❑ Trifling or toying in witchcraft or "spirits" is harmless . ❍T ❍F ❍?

L❑ Seeking wisdom apart from God has consequences .. ❍T ❍F ❍?

M❑ A true prophet of God might have a message of hope and happiness .... ❍T ❍F ❍?

N❑ A false prophet might deliver a message of hope and happiness .... ❍T ❍F ❍?

O❑ A true prophet of God does not deliver messages from their own heart/mind/thoughts .... ❍T ❍F ❍?

P❑ A false prophet proclaims messages from their own heart/mind/thoughts................................ ❍T ❍F ❍?

Q❑ A true prophet of God might have a message of coming judgment, doom, and gloom.............. ❍T ❍F ❍?

R❑ A false prophet might deliver a message of coming judgment, doom, and gloom .... ❍T ❍F ❍?

S❑ A true prophet of God does not deliver messages from selfish interests or desires...................... ❍T ❍F ❍?

T❑ False prophets often profit from what they say .... ❍T ❍F ❍?

U❑ A false prophet delivers messages
from selfish interests and desires .... ❍T ❍F ❍?

V❑ Falsely claiming to speak for God can **reap** [a reward or fruit of labor or works; in a good or bad sense] deadly consequences. ❍T ❍F ❍?

W❑ A false prophet is one who, acting the part of
a divinely inspired prophet, utters falsehoods
under the name of divine prophecies. .... ❍T ❍F ❍?

X❑ The Bible teaches us to beware of false prophets........ ❍T ❍F ❍?

Y❑ I know someone who claimed to represent God,
yet it was determined, discovered, or uncovered they
spoke from their own flesh, not God's Holy Spirit............. ❍T ❍F ❍?

Z❑ I know someone who might be a genuine prophet....... ❍T ❍F ❍?

I know someone who might be a false prophet........... ❍T ❍F ❍?

I believe this/these ❍celebrated, ❍famous, ❍publicly known person(s) is a false prophet:

PERSEVERE Jonah 1:15

20❑ Jonah is a true prophet of God (see page ***44***) .... ❍T ❍F ❍?

21❑ Jonah profited from his prophecy. .... ❍T ❍F ❍?

22❑ This is likely one of the most **curious** [strongly desirous to see what is novel, discover what is unknown; solicitous to see or to know; inquisitive to research] *unanswered* questions in the Bible. We cannot know the mind of Jonah during his **crisis** [the decisive state of things, or the point of time when business, matters, or concerns are at their height and must soon terminate or suffer an important, momentous, or necessary change]. If Jonah knew the Lord gave him unnatural insight into the future, why didn't he jump off the ship without assistance?

I can defend my answer based on: ❍ doctrine ❍ fact ❍ feeling ❍ guess ❍ hypothesis ❍ investigation ❍ judgment ❍ opinion ❍ Scripture ❍ theology ❍ theory (definitions pg ***61–62***). ☆ Worthy of discussion.

Scripture/address: ______________________

Narwhal
Beluga
Blue whale
Humpback whale
Sperm whale

Jonah 1:16 Then the men feared the Lord exceedingly, and offered a sacrifice to the Lord, and made vows.

1❏ Handwrite Jonah 1:16. When a sentence is long, indent the next line as you continue. Remember to start on a new line after each punctuation mark (see page ***64***).

2❏ According to 1:16, what is the result of Jonah going overboard?

A)______________________________

B)______________________________

C)______________________________

3❏ Whom did the men now **fear** [H3372 v fear, be afraid; to stand in awe of; reverence (fear mingled with respect, esteem, and affection); honor: a painful emotion or passion excited by an expectation of evil, or the apprehension of impending danger], and how would you describe your understanding of that kind of fear in your own words?

4❑ What word is used to further describe the **fear** they felt?
_ _ _ _ _ _ _ _ _ _ _ _ _ _ _ , [H1419 *adj* going beyond, surpassing, excelling, outdoing, great in extent, quality, or duration; superabundant in magnitude and extent].

5❑ Let's look back at the last use of the word exceedingly from Jonah 1:10a (see page ***160***). The Hebrew word used is yārē':

> **Then were the men exceedingly afraid,**
> **and said to him** (Jonah)**. Why have you done this?...**

exceedingly [H3373 yārē' *yaw-**ray*** *adj* fear, be afraid, afraid of, stand in awe of, fearing God]

Here in Jonah 1:16a, the Hebrew word used is gādôl:

> **Then the men feared the Lord exceedingly,**
> **and offered a sacrifice...**

exceedingly, [H1419 gādôl *gaw-**dole*** *adj* great in magnitude and extent, in number, in intensity, in sound, in age, in importance: of things, of men, of God himself such as His works, glory, name, mercy, goodness, compassion, etc.; God's great acts of redemption and judgment].

6❑ Read each verse in context, what do you notice that differs between the two Hebrew words transliterated to English as "exceedingly"?

____

____

____

____

____

____

7❑ Did the sailor's belief or faith change, and if so, how?

8❑ What two actions did the sailors take after having "feared the Lord":

1 **offered** [H2076 v to slaughter; kill; sacrifice] **a** _ _ _ _ _ _ _ _ _ [H2077 n the flesh of slain animals] **to the Lord**

2 **and made** [H5087 v to promise to voluntarily do or give something (to God)] _ _ _ _ [H5088 n a promise (to God)**.**

9❑ If the mariners lightened the ship from excess weight (1:5), how valuable might any remaining animal (source of protein) be for their survival?

10❑ It is unlikely the sailors suffered from their sacrifice. ❍T ❍F ❍?

11❑ How did God use Jonah's bad/poor testimony for His good?

12❍ Have you ever made a **vow** [to give, consecrate, or dedicate to God (or a pagan deity) by a solemn promise; a vow is a promise of something to be given or done hereafter; in a moral and religious sense, vows are promises to God, as they appeal to God to witness their sincerity] **or promise** [in a general sense, a declaration, written or verbal, made by one person to another, which binds the person who makes it, either in honor, conscience or law, to do or forbear a certain act specified; a declaration which gives to the person to whom it is made, a right to expect or to claim the performance or forbearance of the act; a binding declaration of something to be done or given for another's benefit; in Scripture, the promise of God is the declaration or assurance which God has given in his word of bestowing blessings on his people. Such assurance resting on the perfect justice, power, benevolence and immutable veracity of God, cannot fail of performance.] to God? If so, share that experience and the end result.

☆ It would be nice to talk with someone about this subject.

Blue whale is the largest animal ever. Giant fossils that were originally believed to be dinosaurs were later identified as ancient whales.

Sperm whales have the largest brain of any animal.

The 1851 classic novel Moby Dick was so named from the writer's experience as a sailor and the evasive sperm whale he named Mocha Dick. Some find its theological symbolism unmatched.

Toothed whales can't chew food, they swallow it whole or in big chunks.

Baleen whales have flexible overlapping plates of keratin which appears like hairy fringe. Keratin is the same substance human hair and fingernails consist of.

In 1970 a recording of whales "singing" sold over 125,000 copies: Songs Of The Humpback Whale - by Dr. Roger Payne.

Twenty-eight African bush elephants combined weigh as much as a single blue whale.

Gray whale have two blowholes that expel water that appears heart-shaped.

Baby blue whale's milk contains about 50% fat, making its texture that of toothpaste.

In 2009 a beluga whale hoisted drowning diver Yang Yun to the water's surface, saving her life.

Inside the head of sperm whale is a very large organ (the spermaceti) which contains a white liquid ancient whalers misidentified as sperm. Spermaceti "wax" is used to make candles, cosmetics, textile products and industrial lubricants.

Humpback whales weighing 60,000 pounds fully jump out of the water.

Gray whales migrate 14,000 miles from Baja to the Arctic and back yearly.

Jonah 1:17 Now the Lord had prepared a great fish to swallow up Jonah. And Jonah was in the belly of the fish three days and three nights.

1❑ Handwrite Jonah 1:17. When a sentence is long, indent the next line as you continue. Remember to start on a new line after each punctuation mark (see page ***64***).

____

____

____

____

____

____

2❑ A random surprise event occurred to Jonah ❍Y ❍N ❍?

3❑ **Now the Lord** [Yehôvâh *yeh-ho-***vaw** [YHWH H3068 n the existing One, self-Existent Eternal] **had** _ _ _ _ _ _ _ _ * [H4487 v to assign, allot; appoint, ordain; constitute]...

4❑ Let's **expound** [to explain; to lay open the meaning; to clear of obscurity; to interpret] **the definition above to get a stronger sense of the meaning and its impact. Underline words that add to your understanding.**

...**assign** [to send or set, allot, designate, appoint for a particular purpose]

...**allot** [to divide or distribute by lot; to give, assign or appoint]

...**appoint** [to fix by decree, order or decision; settle, establish, constitute, ordain; allot, assign or designate; purpose or resolve]

...**ordain** [to set; to establish in a particular office or order; to appoint, decree; to institute; to constitute; to prepare]

...**constitute** [to appoint, compose, depute, empower, enact, establish, fix, form, make, or set; to give formal existence to; to make a thing what it is]

5❏ Jonah was tossed into the sea during a raging storm. He faced almost certain death without someone or something that could and would **intervene** [to come or be between events, persons, points, or time or things; to happen in a way to disturb, cross or interrupt; to interpose or undertake voluntarily for another]......................❍Correct ❍Incorrect ❍?

6❏ If the Bible states "God prepared," is that believable?.. ❍Y ❍N ❍?

7❏ No "fish" is able to swallow an adult human being .... ❍T ❍F ❍?

8❏ Beginning on page ***84***, review then write a *brief* description of:

Omnipotent ____

____

Omnipresent ____

____

Omniscient ____

____

9❏ Through the Lord (the one who exists and Creator of all things), ❏ nothing, ❏ some things occur(s) by **chance** [n an event that happens, falls out or takes place, without being contrived, intended, expected or foreseen; the effect of an unknown cause, or the unusual or unexpected effect of a known cause; accident; casualty; fortuitous event; fortune; an event, good or evil; success or misfortune; luck; possibility of an occurrence; opportunity].
Because He is ❏ Omnipotent, ❏ Omnipresent, and ❏ Omniscient.

10❏ Through the Lord, ❏ nothing, ❏ some things occur(s) by **coincidence** [n the falling or meeting of two or more lines, surfaces, or bodies in the same point; a meeting or happening of events in time; concurrence (a meeting or coming together; union; conjunction; a combination of agents, circumstances or events)]. **(review pg *84*)**
Because God is: ❏ Omnipotent, ❏ Omnipresent, and ❏ Omniscient.

11❑ What had the Lord **prepared**? _ _ _ _ _ _ _ _ _ _ _

12❑ Why? **to** _ _ _ _ _ _ _ **up** [H1104 *v* engulf; to make away with] **Jonah**

13❑ This event was ❑ **natural** [pertaining to, produced or effected by nature; according to the stated course of things; not forced; not far fetched; produced or coming in the ordinary course of things], ❑ **supernatural** [being beyond or exceeding the powers or laws of nature; miraculous. A supernatural event is one that is not produced according to the ordinary or established laws of natural things; supernatural events or miracles can be produced only by the immediate agency of divine power].

14❑ I have personally been ❍ present during, ❍ experienced, or ❍ observed a supernatural event. ....❍Correct ❍Incorrect ❍?

This is what happened:

☆ It would be nice to talk with someone about this subject.

◁ ◁ ◁ PAUSE Jonah 1:17

A❑ In the following cross-references, decide if the verses teach that "in the Lord" things happen by chance, coincidence (definitions pg ***222***) **or providence** [the act of providing or preparing for future use or application; good governance; foresight; timely care; particularly, active foresight, or foresight accompanied with the procurement of what is necessary for future use, or with suitable preparation; a manifestation of divine care, direction or intervention; in theology, the care and superintendence which God exercises over his creatures].
Similar words people use or misuse for providence include: accident, destiny, divine intervention, fate, fluke, fortune, happenstance, luck, one's lot or portion, predestination, and/or predetermination.

Use the blank lines to note questions, thoughts, or anything else you want to share or research.

Genesis 50:20 (✍1450–1410 BC) ❍ *Chance* ❍ *Coinc.* ❍ *Providence*

But as for you, you thought evil against me; but God meant it to good, to bring to pass, as it is this day, to save much people alive.

Proverbs 16:33 (✍1000–900 BC) ❍ *Chance* ❍ *Coinc.* ❍ *Providence*

The lot is cast into the lap; but the whole disposing [verdict; sentence; decree; justice; decision] **thereof is of the Lord.**

Isaiah 46:9 (✍681 BC) ❍ *Chance* ❍ *Coinc.* ❍ *Providence*

Remember the former things of old: for I am God, and there is none else; I am God, and there is none like me, *10* **Declaring the end from the beginning, and from ancient times the things that are not yet done, saying, My counsel shall stand, and I will do all my pleasure:**

Daniel 4:35 (✍535 BC) ❍ *Chance* ❍ *Coinc.* ❍ *Providence*

And all the inhabitants of the earth are reputed as nothing: and he does according to his will in the army of heaven, and among the inhabitants of the earth: and none can stay [strike; hinder] **his hand, or say to him, What do you?**

Romans 8:28 (✍AD 56–57) ❍ *Chance* ❍ *Coinc.* ❍ *Providence*

And we know that all things work together for good to them that love God, to them who are the called according to his purpose.

B❑ Think of something that occurred in your life, which at the time you believed was a coincidence or by chance, but now see the Lord allowed it in your life for a reason (even if you haven't yet figured out the reason):

C❑ It is my belief, in the Lord, ❑ nothing happens ❑ some things happen by ❑ chance or ❑ coincidence.

Because:

I can defend my answer based on: ❍ doctrine ❍ fact ❍ feeling ❍ guess ❍ hypothesis ❍ investigation ❍ judgment ❍ opinion ❍ Scripture ❍ theology ❍ theory (definitions pg ***61—62***). ☆ Worthy of discussion.

Scripture/address:

▷ ▷ ▷ PERSEVERE Jonah 1:17

15❑ Now the Lord had prepared a great _ _ _ _ [H1709 *n* a class of animals subsisting in water; in the sense of squirming, i.e., moving by the vibratory action of the tail] **to swallow up Jonah...**

16❑ Creation, from Genesis 1, is summarized below.

Genesis 1:1 (✍1450–1410 BC)

In the beginning God created the heaven and the earth.

Day 1 Light/Darkness, Day/Night *1:2–5*

Day 2 Made the firmament/Divided the waters; Heaven *1:6–8*

Day 3 Dry land/Earth; Gathered waters/Seas *1:9–10*
Grass/Herb yielding seed; Fruit trees *1:11–13*

Day 4 Two great lights: Sun/Moon; Stars *1:14–19*

Day 5 Moving creatures of the waters/Fowls to fly *1:20*
Great whales/Every living creature that moves *1:21–23*

Day 6 Living creatures, cattle, creeping things, beasts *1:24–25*
Mankind: Male/Female *1:26–31*

❍ Underline references to water and water creatures:

17❑ Creation Day 3: When the land and waters were separated, the waters were called: _ _ _ _

Mankind later classified the waters, i.e., lakes, ponds, oceans, rivers, seas, streams, etc.

18❑ Creation Day 5: "...moving _ _ _ _ _ _ _ _ _ of the waters"

Mankind later classified them as ocean animals, i.e., cuttlefish, dolphin, fish, jellyfish, octopus, penguin, rays, seahorse, sea lion, shark, squid, sea turtle, whale, etc.

19❑ Swimming in a sea or ocean does not concern me ... ❍T ❍F ❍?

20❏ Creation Day 5: **Great whales** are defined as:

Gesenius' Hebrew-Chaldee Lexicon: [a great serpent, a sea monster, a vast fish; Ezekiel 29:3 ***Speak, and say, Thus says the Lord God; Behold, I am against you, Pharaoh king of Egypt, the great dragon that lies in the midst of his rivers, which has said, My river is my own, and I have made it for myself***, Genesis 1:21 ***And God created great whales, and every living creature that moves, which the waters brought forth abundantly, after their kind...***, Job 7:12 ***Am I a sea, or a whale, that you set a watch over me?***, Isaiah 27:1 ***In that day the Lord with his sore and great and strong sword shall punish leviathan the piercing serpent, even leviathan that crooked serpent; and he shall slay the dragon that is in the sea)***; a serpent (Exodus 7:9 ... ***say to Aaron, Take your rod, and cast it before Pharaoh, and it shall become a serpent***, Deuteronomy 32:33 ***Their wine is the poison of dragons, and the cruel venom of asps***, Psalm 91:13 ...***the young lion and the dragon shall you trample under feet***)]

[H8577 *n* intensive from the same as H8565; a marine or land monster, i.e., sea-serpent or jackal; dragon, serpent, whale; a sea monster, a vast fish; a sea or river monster, a crocodile (Ezek 29:3)]. [H8565 *n* from an unused root probably meaning to elongate; a monster (as preternaturally formed=beyond or aside from the common order of nature), i.e., a sea-serpent (or other huge marine animal); outside of water creatures, a jackal (or other hideous land animal).

❍ Underline **animals** [an organized body endowed with life and the power of voluntary motion; a living, sensitive, locomotive body] mentioned in the above definitions.

21❏ Fish, great fish, whale, and great whale are living, breathing animals, creatures of the waters..................❍Correct ❍Incorrect ❍?

22❏ According to the Bible, God created: ❍ dragons ❍ fish ❍ great whales ❍ huge marine animals ❍ marine, sea or river monsters ❍ ocean animals ❍ moving creatures of the waters ❍ sea-serpents ❍ vast/huge fish

23❑ Whales are warm-blooded mammals that live in an aquatic environment. Whales are not fish. They are the largest animals on the planet. Because they breathe through their lungs, they must come to the water's surface to get air through their blowhole. Some whales can hold their breath for an hour and a half! Blue whales can grow to 110 feet/33.5m long. Other large whales are the humpback, fin, right, and sperm. Whales use their horizontal fin to power them up, down, and forward. They birth live young which can weigh up to 6,000 pounds/2722kg. Jonah was **swallowed** [engulfed; to make away with] by a whale:

............................❍Yes/possible ❍No/impossible ❍Maybe/not sure

24❑ Fish have vertical tails that move back and forth, propelling them gracefully through the water. Fish are not mammals. They are cold-blooded and adapt to all temperatures. The largest fish species is the whale shark. It is not a shark—it is a fish with gills. Whale sharks (named long ago only because of their size) grow over 40 feet/12m long. Other large fish are the basking, great white, and tiger shark. Some sharks birth live babies, but most fish lay eggs that survive on their own once hatched. Jonah was swallowed by a shark: ....❍Yes/possible ❍No/impossible ❍Maybe/not sure

25❑ Jonah was swallowed by a fish:

............................❍Yes/possible ❍No/impossible ❍Maybe/not sure

26❑ A whale **subsists** [exists; lives] in water....................... ❍T ❍F ❍?

... and moves by **vibrating** [moving to and fro] its tail .... ❍T ❍F ❍?

A shark subsists in water .... ❍T ❍F ❍?

... and moves by vibrating its tail .... ❍T ❍F ❍?

A fish subsists in water .... ❍T ❍F ❍?

... but doesn't move by vibrating its tail.............................. ❍T ❍F ❍?

27❑ The creature that swallowed Jonah is something that exists in water and moves by use of its tail................ ❍T ❍F ❍?

28❑ The thing that swallowed Jonah is further described as **a** _ _ _ _ _ _ [H1419 *adj* going beyond, surpassing, excelling, outdoing, great in extent, quality, or duration; superabundant in magnitude and extent] **fish.**

29❑ Notice the missing word (above) is an **adjective** [a word following a noun that expresses a quality of the thing named, or something attributed to it, or to limit or define it, or to specify or describe a thing, as distinct from something else. It is also called an attributive or attribute]. It is used to define the size, design, qualities, etc., and describes a:

❍ natural marine animal ❍ supernatural marine animal

I can defend my answer based on: ❍ doctrine ❍ fact ❍ feeling ❍ guess ❍ hypothesis ❍ investigation ❍ judgment ❍ opinion ❍ Scripture ❍ theology ❍ theory (definitions pg ***61-62***). ☆ Worthy of discussion.

*Scripture/address:*____

30❑ **And Jonah was in the** _ _ _ _ _ _ [H4578 *n* womb; internal organs; inward parts; bowels; intestines] **of the fish three days and three nights**.

Jonah entered the mouth, throat, then belly of the animal ..... ❍T ❍F ❍?

31❑ **FISH:** The whale shark (named for its size) is the world's largest living fish. It has a wide flat head, wide mouth (up to five feet/1.5m), large gills, distinctive patterned white spots, a white belly, wide-set eyes, and about 3,000 teeth (even though it is a filter feeder). Whale sharks measure up to 41 feet/12.5m long, have a girth to 23 feet/7m, and weigh up to 47,400 pounds/21.5 metric tons. They feed on small prey and consume up to 660 pounds/300kg of food daily. They sometimes bob up and down vertically to feed. To clear or flush its gills, they employ a coughing method. Whale sharks are known to ram vessels at sea but are more likely to be struck by one while feeding. They dive to depths of 2,300 feet/701m, are slow-moving, and are *not* aggressive which is why scuba divers sometimes approach them.

A giant fish might be able to swallow a human .... ❍T ❍F ❍?

A whale shark might be able to swallow a human .... ❍T ❍F ❍?

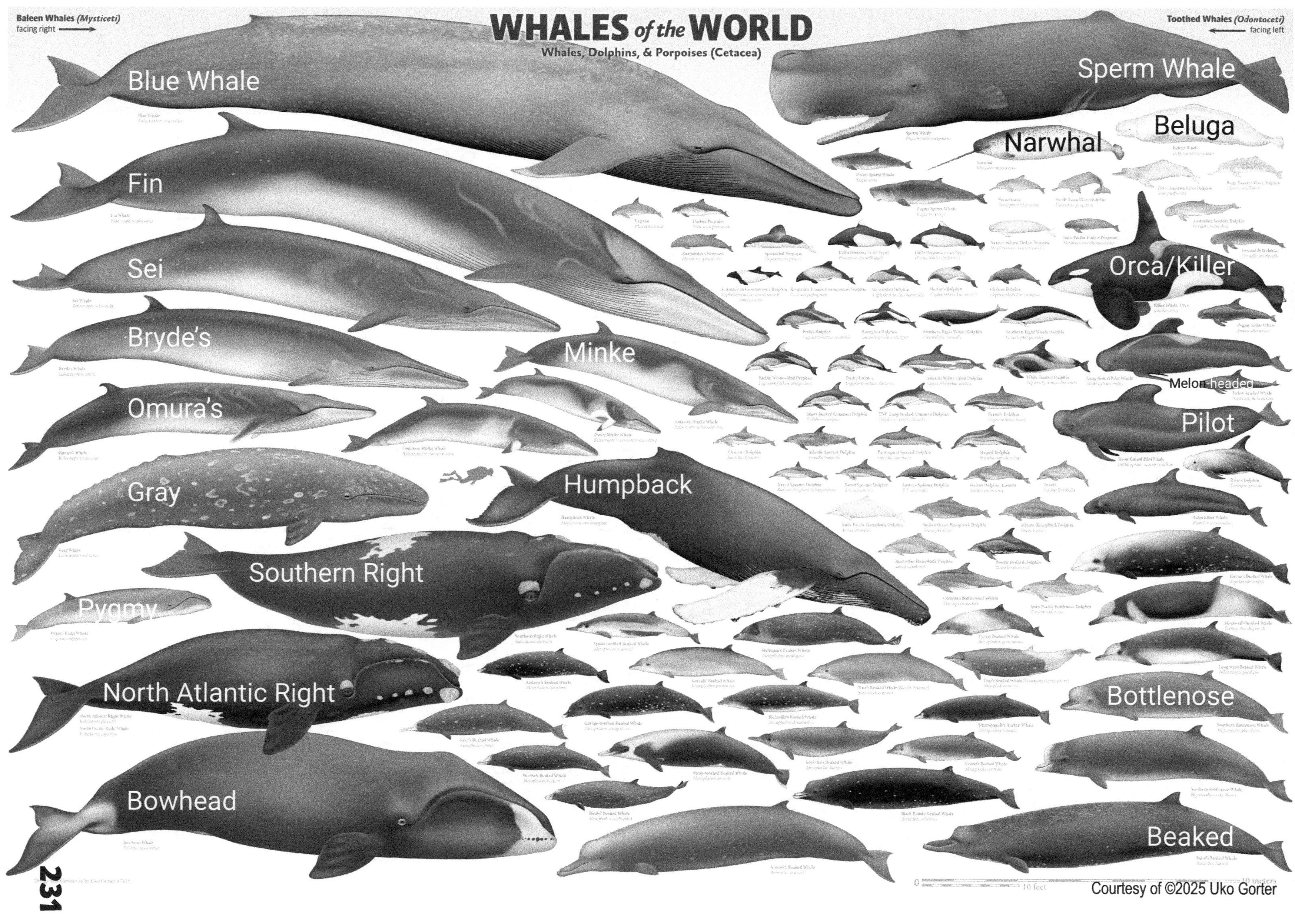

WHALES of the WORLD
Whales, Dolphins, & Porpoises (Cetacea)
Baleen Whales (Mysticeti) facing right
Toothed Whales (Odontoceti) facing left
Blue Whale
Fin
Sei
Bryde's
Omura's
Minke
Gray
Humpback
Southern Right
Pygmy
North Atlantic Right
Bowhead
Sperm Whale
Narwhal
Beluga
Orca/Killer
Melon-headed
Pilot
Bottlenose
Beaked
Courtesy of ©2025 Uko Gorter

32❑ Marine mammal illustrator Uko Gorter, *www.ukogorter.com*, kindly granted special permission for the "Whales of the World" copyrighted graphic to be shown on the previous page. It depicts all known species of whales, dolphins, and porpoises *(Cetacea)*. They are drawn to scale at average adult lengths. Unless indicated, preference was given to show males, particularly in the toothed whales. The baleen whales *(mysticetes)* face right, and toothed whales *(odontocetes)* face left.

❍ Draw a circle around the human to gain perspective.

WHALE: There are ninety-one (91) species of Cetaceans, which are classified as: 1) dolphins, 2) porpoises, and 3) whales. Of them, fifteen (15) species are *mysticetes* (whales with baleen plates instead of teeth), and seventy-six (76) species are *odontocetes* (whales with teeth).

Put a checkmark by whales you have observed ❍ in person, ❍ by computer, ❍ on TV, or ❍ other media *(listed largest to smallest)*:

Baleen plate whales: ❍ Blue Whale *(Balaenoptera musculus)* 98'/30m ❍ Finback or Fin Whale *(Balaenoptera physalus)* 85'/26m ❍ Humpback Whale *(Megaptera novaeangliae)* 60'/18.2m ❍ Bowhead Whale *(Balaena mysticetus)* 59' /18m ❍ Right Whales 52'/15.8 m ❍ Sei Whale *(Balaenoptera borealis)* 52' ❍ Gray Whale *(Eschrichtius robustus)* 49' /15m ❍ Bryde's Whale *(Balaenoptera brydei)* 46'/14m ❍ Minke *(Balaenoptera acutorostrata)* 35'/10.7m

Toothed whales: ❍ Sperm Whale *(Physeter macrocephalus)* 79'/24m ❍ Bottlenose Whales 37'/11.3m ❍ Orca/Killer *(Orcinus orca) (which is actually a dolphin)* 32' /9.75m ❍ Beaked Whales 23'/7m ❍ Pilot Whales 20'/6m ❍ Narwhal Whale *(Monodon monoceros)* 18'/5.5m ❍ Beluga Whale *(Delphinapterus leucas)* 15/4.6m ❍ Melon headed *(Peponocephala electra)*, 9'/2.7m

2❑ Some whales have a mouth large enough to contain *many* humans but have small passageways leading to the throat, esophagus, and stomach. For example, the giant blue whale's mouth is huge, about 20 feet/6m long, but its throat is about the size of a basketball.

The bowhead's mouth is bigger than *a bedroom,* measuring up to 8'/2.4m wide, 12'/3.7m high, and 16' long/4.9m. But, as a baleen only small crustaceans like krill, shrimp, and capepods can pass through.

The mouth of a sperm whale can measure up to 6.5 feet/2m wide and 4.5 feet/1.4m tall. They have teeth on the lower jaw only and swallow their prey whole. Their throat is large enough to contain a human. Its favorite food? Giant squid which can grow to 43 feet/13m.

Unless supernatural, it is difficult to believe a:

...blue whale could swallow *and **retain*** [hold or keep in possession; not to lose or part with or dismiss; hold from escape] a human ... ❍Y ❍N ❍?

...bowhead whale could swallow *and retain* a human........ ❍Y ❍N ❍?

...sperm whale could swallow *and retain* a human .... ❍Y ❍N ❍?

33❑ Some whales can swim to depths of 6562 feet/2000m below the water's surface (sea level).

To date, the world free diving (diving without an oxygen tank) record is 400 feet/122m, done in three minutes and 34 seconds. Diving to extreme depths causes body tissues to absorb nitrogen. If a diver ascends to the water's surface too quickly, nitrogen forms bubbles in the diver's bloodstream and tissues. The result is decompression sickness, *aka* "the bends" (named from bending over in excruciating pain). Symptoms include blackouts, clouded thinking, difficulty breathing, fatigue, joint, muscle or tendon aches, swelling, inflammation or pain, heart issues, numbness, paralysis, poor coordination or balance, rash, vertigo, and/or weakness. Without immediate medical attention, it can lead to paralysis or death.

If Jonah was retained inside a fish or whale, and it dove deep, it seems possible he suffered from "the bends"....... ❍T ❍F ❍?

 Date: __________

34❑ Fish and whales have almost constant movement. They vibrate their tail up and down or side to side, twist their body left then right, breach the water's surface, and sometimes make graceful 360° corkscrew maneuvers.

If Jonah was retained inside a fish or whale, it is likely the "roller coaster ride" would *not* affect him.................................... ❍T ❍F ❍?

This type of experience would *not* affect me.................... ❍T ❍F ❍?

35❑ Depending on the stomach of the fish or whale Jonah found himself in, he would encounter whole and partially digested algae, amphipods, barnacle, clams, crab, crayfish, fish lice, herring, isopods, krill, lobster, molluscs, octopus, oysters, pill bugs, scallops, sea monkeys, seaweed, shrimp, slugs, snail, squid (including neon squid which could light up the area), water fleas, and/or woodlice.

Would this "fish/whale soup" gross you out? .... ❍Y ❍N ❍?

36❑ A fish or whale's stomach contains acidic gastric juices such as bile (cholic acid conjugated with taurine) enzymes, hydrochloric acid, or pepsin, which are necessary for digestion.

Imagine how a fish/whale's stomach "acid wash" might affect Jonah's hair, skin, nails, and/or ability to breathe, hear, feel, see, etc.):

____

____

____

____

____

37❑ Without supernatural intervention, the decomposition of animal and plant matter inside the stomach of a fish or whale could create high levels of natural methane gas. A gas that is highly flammable, and when pressurized even at low concentration levels, presents the risk of explosion.

The results of a lack of oxygen or from methane poisoning are brain injury, collapse, coma, convulsions, decreased vision, dizziness, fainting, fatigue, headache, heart issues, impaired alertness, loss of balance, memory loss, nausea, numbness, rapid breathing, slurred speech, suffocation, unconsciousness, vomiting, weakness, and/or death.

Have you ever experienced a lack of oxygen? .... ❍Yes ❍No ❍?

...methane gas poisoning?.. ❍Yes ❍No ❍?

...carbon monoxide poisoning? .... ❍Yes ❍No ❍?

38❑ In 1891, sailor James Barley shared graphic details of having survived thirty-six hours inside a sperm whale near the Falkland Islands. By 1914, historians and scholars were able to "fact-check" Barley's story and prove it a hoax.

In 2019, *a photographer* captured the moment Rainer Schimpf's head and torso were caught up in the mouth of a Bryde's whale. Less than two seconds later, he was spewed out.

In 2021, *a fellow crewman witnessed* Michael Packard, a commercial lobster diver, as he was **engulfed** [absorbed in a deep abyss] by a humpback whale. Fortunately, thirty seconds later, Michael was spit out, suffering only minor injuries.

February 2025, in the Strait of Magellan, *while being filmed* by his father, Adrián Simancas *and his kayak* were briefly caught up in a humpback whale's mouth. *(Video can be viewed on websites)*

Modern historical records report humans have been **swallowed** [engulfed; made away with; taken into the stomach] by large ocean animals (with eye-witnesses as proof)............................... ❍T ❍F ❍?

39❑ In these examples, the fish/whale retained the human. ❍T ❍F ❍?

40❑ And Jonah was in the belly of the fish _ _ _ _ _ days [H3117 *n* as opposed to night; 24 hour period] **and _ _ _ _ _ nights** [H3915 *n* a twist away of the light; as opposed to day]**.**

If you are familiar with the New Testament, what is **significant** [*adj* standing as a sign of something; expressive or representative of some fact or event] about the scripture above?

I can defend my answer based on: ❍ doctrine ❍ fact ❍ feeling ❍ guess ❍ hypothesis ❍ investigation ❍ judgment ❍ opinion ❍ Scripture ❍ theology ❍ theory (definitions pg ***61—62***). ☆ Worthy of discussion.

Scripture/address: ______________________________

◁ ◁ ◁ PAUSE Jonah 1:17

A❏ Underline the first use of the word "miracle" in the Bible:

Exodus 7:8 (✍1450—1410 BC)

And the Lord spoke to Moses and to Aaron, saying, *9* **When Pharaoh shall speak to you, saying, Show a miracle for you: then you shall say to Aaron, Take your rod, and cast it before Pharaoh, and it shall become a serpent.** *10* **And Moses and Aaron went in to Pharaoh, and they did so as the Lord had commanded: and Aaron cast down his rod before Pharaoh, and before his servants, and it became a serpent.**

miracle [H4159 *n* a beautiful or splendid deed; a wonder or wonderful thing as a special display of God's power; a sign or token of a future event, used of divine acts, signs of divine authority; it is often used of the sign given by a prophet to cause that which has been predicted or promised to be believed; used of miracles performed by God and by those sent by Him. In theology, an event or effect contrary to the established constitution and course of things, or a deviation from the known laws of nature; a supernatural event. Miracles can be wrought (worked) only by Almighty power]

B❏ Interestingly, the Hebrew word for miracle, môpet, is pronounced *mo-**faith*** (not the meaning but the pronunciation). The pronunciation is a great, simple to remember memory aide: ***more-faith***!

How might a miracle of God increase a person's faith?

C❏ ❍ I can personally testify as a witness of a miracle or ❍ "This" happened to someone I ❍ believe ❍ know ❍ trust:

☆ It would be nice to talk with someone about this subject.

D❍ Read the events after Mary and Martha's brother Lazarus died. Circle the number of days he was dead.

John 11:32–45 (✍AD 55–56)

32 **Then when Mary was come where Jesus was, and saw him,**
she fell down at his feet, saying to him, Lord, if you had been
here, my brother had not died. *33* **When Jesus therefore saw her**
weeping, and the Jews also weeping which came with her, he
groaned in the spirit, and was troubled. *34* **And said, Where have**
you laid him? They said to him, Lord, come and see. *35* **Jesus**
wept. *36* **Then said the Jews, Behold how he loved him!** *37* **And**
some of them said, Could not this man, which opened the eyes
of the blind, have caused that even this man should not have
died? *38* **Jesus therefore again groaning in himself comes to the**
grave. It was a cave, and a stone lay upon it. *39* **Jesus said, Take**
you away the stone. Martha, the sister of him that was dead,
said to him, Lord, by this time he stinks: for he has been dead
four days. *40* **Jesus saith to her, Said I not to you, that, if you**
would believe, you should see the glory of God? *41* **Then they**
took away the stone from the place where the dead was laid.
And Jesus lifted up his eyes, and said, Father, I thank you that
you have heard me. *42* **And I knew that you hear me always: but**
because of the people which stand by I said it, that they may
believe that you have sent me. *43* **And when he thus had spoken,**
he cried with a loud voice, Lazarus, come forth. *44* **And he that**
was dead came forth, bound hand and foot with graveclothes:
and his face was bound about with a napkin. Jesus said to them,
Loose him, and let him go. *45* **Then many of the Jews which**
came to Mary, and had seen the things which Jesus did, believed
on him.

Date: ____________

E❏ The word **dead** means: [adj deprived or destitute of life; that state of a being in which the organs of motion and life have ceased to perform their functions and have become incapable of performing them, or of being restored to a state of activity; unable to be revived; without life; inanimate (not animated). Note: Spiritual death describes a person who is destitute of the grace of God freely offered, and instead has chosen to remain under the power of sin. One who is not born again—John 3]

F❏ Was Lazarus **dead** [unable to be revived]?........................ ❍Y ❍N ❍?

G❏ Could anything less than a miracle resurrect Lazarus?❍Y ❍N ❍?

H❏ Were eye witnesses able to testify of his death?......... ❍Y ❍N ❍?

I❏ It is easy to deny the miracle of Lazarus' **resurrection** [a rising again; revival (return, recall, or recovery to life from death)] ...... ❍T ❍F ❍?

J❏ I personally believe Lazarus was raised from the dead ❍T ❍F ❍?

K❏ This event was a sign of God's divine authority .... ❍T ❍F ❍?

L❏ Lazarus' resurrection increased the faith of Believers.. ❍T ❍F ❍?

M❏ God used the miracle of Lazarus' resurrection to **inspire** [infuse or suggest ideas or monitions supernaturally; to communicate divine instructions to the mind] more faith .... ❍T ❍F ❍?

N❏ If someone was indeed dead, unable to be **revived,** [returned to life and vigor, reanimated], it would take a miracle for that person to be **resurrected** [a rising again; chiefly, the revival of the dead of the human race, or their return from the grave] back to life .... ❍T ❍F ❍?

O❏ Miracles occur **frequently** [often; many times; at short intervals; commonly] .... ❍T ❍F ❍?

P❏ Humans can **absolutely** [completely; without restriction or limitation; without condition; positively] ask God for a miracle❍T ❍F ❍?

Q❏ Some people can make miracles happen .... ❍T ❍F ❍?

R❏ I know someone who can make miracles happen........ ❍T ❍F ❍?

PERSEVERE Jonah 1:17

41❑ How does the account of Lazarus in John 11 add value or understanding to Jonah 1?

____

____

____

____

____

____

42❑ The lack of eye witness testimony, historical archives, or scientific facts and research make it ❍ difficult ❍ impossible to believe Jonah could survive in the "great fish" for three days and three nights unless you have faith in God's word alone ..... ❍T ❍F ❍?

43❑ The only way Jonah could survive in the belly of a fish for three days and three nights is by a miracle of God .... ❍T ❍F ❍?

44❑ It is possible Jonah ❑ fainted, ❑ was rendered unconscious, ❑ died, in the belly of the fish .... ❍T ❍F ❍?

45❑ I have personally experienced an act of God too supernatural to be anything other than a true miracle?..... ❍Y ❍N ❍?

46❑ *Matthew 12:38—41* (✍AD 60—65)

38 **Then certain of the scribes and of the Pharisees answered, saying, Master, we would see a sign from you.** *39* **But he** (Jesus) **answered and said to them, An evil and adulterous generation seeks after a sign; and there shall no sign be given to it, but the sign of the prophet Jonas:** (Jonah) *40* **For as Jonas was three days and three nights in the whale's belly; so shall the Son of**

man be three days and three nights in the heart of the earth. *41* **The men of Nineveh shall rise in judgment with this generation, and shall condemn it: because they repented at the preaching of Jonas; and, behold, a greater than Jonas is here.**

Religious leaders wanted **a** _ _ _ _

47❑ Handwrite Jesus' answer from Matthew 12:39-41. It will help you focus on what Jesus believed. When a sentence is long, indent the next line as you continue. Remember to start on a new line after each punctuation mark (see page ***64***).

48❑ Jesus addresses the Jewish religious leaders by pointing out they and their generation (the Israelites, the nation of the Jewish people) were evil and adulterous. Even though miracles of God were evident, the hardened Jews would not believe Jesus was God's anointed messenger, the Messiah.

Rather than perform a miracle by demand, Jesus pointed them back to the _ _ _ Testament book of Jonah. This generation of Jews is stubborn and hard-hearted, like the Pharaoh of Egypt, who refused to believe though many miracles and signs were given. You can read of Pharaoh's attempt to annihilate a generation of Jews, the plagues of Egypt, and the results of ignoring God in:

❍ *Exodus Chapters 1 through 12* (✍1415–1410 BC)

49❑ How many days and nights was Jonah in the belly of the fish/whale? ....❍1 ❍2 ❍3 ❍4 ❍5 ❍6 ❍7 ❍8 ❍9 ❍10

50❑ How many days and nights was Jesus in the tomb? ....❍1 ❍2 ❍3 ❍4 ❍5 ❍6 ❍7 ❍8 ❍9 ❍10

51❑ The phrase "three days and three nights" can be understood as a portion or any part of the day or night. .... ❍T ❍F ❍?

52❑ Jonah was a "prisoner" in the belly of the whale. .... ❍T ❍F ❍?

53❑ Jesus was a "prisoner" in the heart of the earth. .... ❍T ❍F ❍?

54❑ Jonah paid a price for his own sins. .... ❍T ❍F ❍?

55❑ Jesus paid a price for his own sins. .... ❍T ❍F ❍?

56❑ A prophet of God relays the Word of God as His representative on earth. .... ❍T ❍F ❍?

57❑ A prophet of God *is sometimes* used to foretell future events given by divine revelation from God. .... ❍T ❍F ❍?

58❑ Some prophets of God are used in healing others. .... ❍T ❍F ❍?

59❑ Some prophets of God are used in performing miracles. ❍T ❍F ❍?

60❑ Jonah was a prophet called to preach to the lost .... ❍T ❍F ❍?

61❑ Jesus was a prophet called to preach to the lost .... ❍T ❍F ❍?

62❑ Although we covered this earlier, there is more to learn:

❍ *Deuteronomy 18:18—19* (✍1407—1406 BC)

18 **I will raise them up a Prophet** [inspired man] **from among their brethren, like to you, and will put my words in his mouth; and he shall speak to them all that I shall command him.** *19* **And it shall come to pass, that whosoever will not hearken** [hear; listen; obey] **to my words which he shall speak in my name, I will require it of him.**

Is Jesus the prophet spoken of in Deuteronomy 18:18? Explain:

What does Deuteronomy 18:19 mean? Explain:

☆ It would be nice to talk with someone about this subject.

63❑ Going back to Matthew 12, finish Jesus' statement to the non-believing Jewish religious leaders:

Matthew 12:39b **...and there shall _ _ sign be given to it, but the sign of the _ _ _ _ _ _ _ _ Jonas:** (Jonah) *40* **For as Jonas was three days and three nights in the whale's** [*G2785 n* a huge fish, as gaping (opening the mouth wide) for prey; whale; a sea-monster] **belly;** [*G2836 n* hollow; a cavity, especially the abdomen; figuratively, the heart; by implication, the womb (the place where the fetus is conceived and nourished until birth); the stomach; the gullet (the passage in the neck of an animal by which food and liquids are taken into the stomach, the esophagus); sometimes used of the innermost part of a man, the soul, heart, as the seat of thought, feeling, and choice] **so** [*G3779 adv* in this way, referring to what precedes or follows, in the manner spoken of, in the way described, in the way it was done, in this manner, in such a manner, thus; consequently; so after that, after or in this manner; as, even so; for all that; like; likewise; no more; on this fashion; so in like manner; thus; equivalent to matters being thus arranged, under these circumstances, in such a condition of things; it prepares the way for what follows] **shall the Son of man be three days and three nights in the heart of the earth.**

64❑ Jesus was obligated to show/reveal a new or special "sign" to those who opposed and did not believe him .... ❍True ❍False ❍?

65❑ Jesus believes the historical account/story of Jonah is **literal** [according to the letter; real; not figurative, not representing something else nor metaphorical (which is the opposite of literal) .... ❍T ❍F ❍?

66❑ Jonah was in the belly of the whale .... ❍T ❍F ❍?

67❑ Jonah and Jonas are one-and-the-same person......... ❍T ❍F ❍?

68❑ Jonah was a prophet of God. .... ❍T ❍F ❍?

69❑ Jesus is a prophet of God, yet God with us. .... ❍T ❍F ❍?

70❑ The author of Jonah Chapter 1 is revealed:................. ❍T ❍F ❍?

71❑ The book of Jonah is written by someone who has **intimate** [within; inmost; inward; internal; near; close; close in friendship or acquaintance; one to whom the thoughts are entrusted without reserve, familiar] **knowledge.**

Go back to Jonah 1 (page **7**). Bullet list things Jonah did that ❍prove or ❍disprove he is the author of Jonah Chapter 1:

- ____________________
- ____________________
- ____________________
- ____________________
- ____________________
- ____________________
- ____________________
- ____________________
- ____________________
- ____________________
- ____________________
- ____________________
- ____________________
- ____________________
- ____________________
- ____________________
- ____________________
- ____________________
- ____________________

72❑ According to a 1417 AD manuscript at the National Library of Paris, University of Paris Catholic professor Stephen Langton divided the Bible (Old and New) into chapters around 1204 AD.

Dividing the *Old* Testament chapters into verses is believed to be the work of Jewish Rabbi "Nathan" in 1448 AD. While work in the *New* Testament is attributed to scholar-printer Robert Estienne Stephanus in 1551 AD.

If I were to divide the verses and paragraphs of Jonah chapter 1:

I would keep Jonah 1:17 as the last verse of the chapter. ❍Y ❍N ❍?
I would merge Jonah 1:17 into Jonah 2:1 .... ❍Y ❍N ❍?

Record today's date at the bottom of this page if you have completely finished (no blank unanswered areas).

Look back at page ***19***. What date did you begin this study?________

How many days did this study keep you "Busy in the Bible? _______

This concludes your in-depth study of Jonah

♡ ***Wow!***

♡ ***You did it!***

♡ ***You finished what you started!***

Coming up next? See what you've retained ➜

Use a pencil so you can erase when needed. Choose the best or most biblically correct answer(s) to each question. You can pick more than one answer, but there might be only one "best-right" answer. It could be *all* in the set are correct.

The goal of this test is to see how much you have retained from your time in God's word. Why not see how many questions you can answer correctly without assistance? Stuck? It's an open-book test, so look back.

1 "Story" means a written
A ❍ Non-serious tale
B ❍ Fable of something fake
C ❍ Account of history
D ❍ Recital of events, facts

2 The Book of Jonah is
A ❍ A story
B ❍ Unreal, fiction/fake
C ❍ Imagery/imagination
D ❍ A myth/folklore

3 The Book of Jonah is
A ❍ A feigned story or tale
B ❍ Evidence of actual events
C ❍ Intended to instruct
D ❍ Intended to amuse

4 Non-fiction means:
A ❍ Fictitious/fake
B ❍ Non-judgmental
C ❍ Not-fake
D ❍ Non-fact

5 The Tortoise and the Hare:
A ❍ Teaches about animals
B ❍ Lesson: win at all costs
C ❍ Slow and steady wins
D ❍ Reminds you to rest

6 Prayer:
A ❍ Is telling God what to do
B ❍ Demands–close your eyes
C ❍ Must be spoken forcefully
D ❍ Is talking to God

7 Coloring is:
A ❍ Calming and creative
B ❍ Empty and meaningless
C ❍ Therapeutic
D ❍ Childish kid stuff

8 A.D. before/after dates mean
A ❍ After Death
B ❍ In the year of our Lord
C ❍ Anno Domini
D ❍ Almost Done

9 B.C. before/after dates mean
A ❍ Because/cause
B ❍ Been crucified
C ❍ Believed correct
D ❍ Before the birth of Christ

10 During the time of Jonah,
A ❍ Events in Amos occurred
B ❍ Events in Micah occurred
C ❍ Events in Hosea occurred
D ❍ Events in Isaiah occurred

11 Hope is closely aligned to:
A ❍ Angst
B ❍ Confidence
C ❍ Expectation
D ❍ Wish

12 Jonah's name means:
A ❍ Darling
B ❍ Daring
C ❍ Dope
D ❍ Dove

13 The author of Jonah is:
A ❍ Jonah
B ❍ Not revealed
C ❍ The shipmaster
D ❍ The great fish

14 Jeroboam II did:
A ❍ Good
B ❍ Nothing
C ❍ Evil
D ❍ More than any other

15 In Jonah, "lots" means:
A ❍ A lot
B ❍ A piece/plot of land
C ❍ Sticks, stones, dice
D ❍ Choices

16 i.e. means:
A ❍ Interesting effects
B ❍ I estimate
C ❍ That is
D ❍ Latin for: in effect

17 e.g. means:
A ❍ For example
B ❍ Example given
C ❍ Exercise grace
D ❍ Illustration given

18 The "word" of the Lord means:
A ❍ Discourse
B ❍ Precept
C ❍ Saying
D ❍ Speech

19 God uses His word through:
A ❍ Hearing
B ❍ Reading
C ❍ Seeing
D ❍ Studying

20 *aka* means:
A ❍ Again know all
B ❍ Also known as
C ❍ Ask knock act
D ❍ Ask know all

21 Old Testament books:
A ❍ Amittai
B ❍ Jonah
C ❍ Michael
D ❍ Micah

22 Biblical meditation includes:
A ❍ Babbling
B ❍ Complaints
C ❍ Communication
D ❍ Reflection

23 Holy Ghost is the same as:
A ❍ A force
B ❍ A spirit of the deceased
C ❍ Holy Spirit
D ❍ Superpowers

24 If contrary to God's Word,
A ❍ Accept it
B ❍ It's the Holy Spirit
C ❍ Proceed
D ❍ Pause, pray, pass it up

25 The word "literally" means:
A ❍ Litter ally
B ❍ As they are
C ❍ Close adherence
D ❍ Real, not figurative

26 Question things to learn:
A ❍ How to annoy people
B ❍ How things work
C ❍ To understand
D ❍ That you're always right

27 Philosophy can be:
A ❍ Bad/wrong/worldly
B ❍ An explanation of things
C ❍ An investigation of causes
D ❍ A quest to understand God

28 Feelings are:
A ❍ Facts
B ❍ The effect of truth
C ❍ An effect of emotions
D ❍ A reaction to guessing

29 Guess is the same as:
A ❍ Opinion without knowledge
B ❍ Conjecture
C ❍ Evidence
D ❍ Opinion at random

30 Theology is the:
A ❍ Assumption of reasoning
B ❍ Theory of truth
C ❍ Science of God
D ❍ Basis of reasoning

31 Doctrine is:
A ❍ Doubt taught by Masters
B ❍ Teaching by an instructor
C ❍ A degree awarded Pastors
D ❍ Whatever is taught as true

32 Nineveh was a city in:
A ❍ Assyria
B ❍ Bethlehem
C ❍ Eden
D ❍ Tigris

33 Wickedness is described as:
A ❍ Virtue
B ❍ Injurious
C ❍ Evil thinking
D ❍ Displeasing to God

34 Omnipotent means:
A ❍ Unlimited power
B ❍ Unlimited presence
C ❍ Unlimited knowledge
D ❍ Universal sovereignty

35 Believe means to
A ❍ Accept anything stated
B ❍ Put your trust in
C ❍ Have special knowledge
D ❍ Think something to be true

36 Belief can include:
A ❍ Internal impressions
B ❍ Arguments for/against
C ❍ Reason
D ❍ Possibility of doubt

37 Faith requires:
A ❍ Scientific proof
B ❍ Confidence to commit
C ❍ Dependence upon beliefs
D ❍ Reliance on knowledge

38 Weather is controlled by:
A ❍ Human intervention
B ❍ Meteorologists
C ❍ God
D ❍ Climate change

39 Supernatural means:
A ❍ Normal/typical
B ❍ Miraculous
C ❍ Exceeding laws of nature
D ❍ Natural superpowers

40 Category 5 winds exceed:
A ❍ 95 mph
B ❍ 110 mph
C ❍ 129 mph
D ❍ 156 mph

41 These words mean the same:
A ❍ Sailor, Salty
B ❍ Mariner, Pilot
C ❍ Seaman, Captain
D ❍ Sailor, Mariner

42 These words mean the same:
A ❍ Cyclone, Hurricane
B ❍ Typhoon, Cyclone
C ❍ Storm, Circular winds
D ❍ Encircling "coil of snake"

43 God's name is:
A ❍ I Exist
B ❍ I Am Created
C ❍ I Tried
D ❍ I Am

44 God—*Elohim* can refer to:
A ❍ The gods of idols
B ❍ The gods of heathens
C ❍ A false god
D ❍ The Supreme true God

45 Mindful awareness is:
A ❍ Emotion
B ❍ Intentional Emotion
C ❍ Feeling
D ❍ Passion

46 The word "culture":
A ❍ Means biblical gardening
B ❍ Only appears in King James
C ❍ Exists in modern Bibles
D ❍ Is not in Hebrew scrolls

47 Biblical Hebrew includes:
A ❍ Periods, commas, etc.
B ❍ Capital letters
C ❍ Only lowercase letters
D ❍ Emoji's

48 Expounding scripture includes:
A ❍ Interpreting
B ❍ Explaining
C ❍ Unfolding significance
D ❍ Hermeneutics

49 Context considers:
A ❍ Nearby words, phrases
B ❍ Passages before or after
C ❍ Related chapters, verses
D ❍ Opinion

50 Let scripture...
A ❍ Be added to or edited
B ❍ Serve as its commentary
C ❍ Interpret itself
D ❍ Determine definitions

51 Etymology is:
A ❍ Figures of speech
B ❍ An explanation of mology
C ❍ Advanced philology
D ❍ The origins of words

52 Wares and "this" are the same:
A ❍ Abbreviation of wariness
B ❍ Utensils
C ❍ Cargo
D ❍ Merchandise

53 The word "plea" means:
A ❍ Urgent prayer
B ❍ Petition, formal request
C ❍ Zealous solicitation
D ❍ Entreaty, earnest request

54 Jonah's shipmaster was:
A ❍ A biblical Believer
B ❍ A god-fearing man
C ❍ A skeptic
D ❍ Superstitious

55 Discern means:
A ❍ To separate by the eye
B ❍ To distinguish
C ❍ To see or understand
D ❍ To make a distinction

56 Evil means:
A ❍ Bad thinking and acting
B ❍ Displeasing to God
C ❍ Destructive
D ❍ Injurious

57 Yehovah *(Lord)* means:
A ❍ Healer
B ❍ The existing One
C ❍ Eternal
D ❍ Self-existent

58 Interrogate means to:
A ❍ Examine by questioning
B ❍ Ask
C ❍ Seek answers
D ❍ Enter the gate

59 Hebrew means:
A ❍ One from the other side
B ❍ The man who brews
C ❍ An Israelite
D ❍ From beyond Euphrates

60 "Fear the Lord" means:
A ❍ He's gonna get you
B ❍ Respect, value
C ❍ Be in awe of
D ❍ Tremble

61 Humble means:
A ❍ Not return injuries
B ❍ Bend the knee, bow down
C ❍ Haughty
D ❍ Submit to another

62 Desperate means:
A ❍ Composed
B ❍ Irretrievable
C ❍ Lost hope of recovery
D ❍ Without hope

63 Events of Jonah occurred:
A ❍ 775 BC
B ❍ 700-786 BC
C ❍ 786-760 BC
D ❍ 775-700 BC

64 Messages of true prophets:
A ❍ Bring hope
B ❍ Heap profits
C ❍ Predict doom/gloom
D ❍ Warn of judgment

65 A vow is a:
A ❍ Voluntary promise
B ❍ Breach
C ❍ Solemn promise
D ❍ Violation

66 The days of Creation are:
A ❍ 1=Dry land/Earth
B ❍ 3=Mankind
C ❍ 5=Water creatures
D ❍ 2=Divided waters/Heaven

67 Miracle means:
A ❍ More faith
B ❍ Beautiful/splendid deed
C ❍ Ordinary/normal/common
D ❍ Sign of divine authority

68 Dead means:
A ❍ Destitute of God's grace
B ❍ Incapable of life functions
C ❍ Unable to be revived
D ❍ Less lively

69 Omnipresent means:
A ❍ Unlimited power
B ❍ Unlimited presence
C ❍ Unlimited knowledge
D ❍ No boundaries

70 Voluntary emotional response:
A ❍ Emotion
B ❍ Intentional Emotion
C ❍ Feeling
D ❍ Passion

71 Persevere means:
A ❍ Persist
B ❍ Pursue steadily
C ❍ Don't quit
D ❍ Discontinue

72 To cast forth is like:
A ❍ Flinging something/one
B ❍ Hurling
C ❍ Casting a javelin spear
D ❍ Catching a fish

73 To retire can mean:
A ❍ Advancement
B ❍ Withdrawal from notice
C ❍ Being withdrawn
D ❍ Secluded from public life

74 A biblical "Believer":
A ❍ Trusts the truth of God
B ❍ Trusts their instincts alone
C ❍ Doubts Bible text
D ❍ Is superstitious

75 If I have discernment I might:
A ❍ Distinguish things
B ❍ Understand differences
C ❍ Properly discriminate
D ❍ Be brainless

76 The word "evil" means:
A ❍ Virtuous
B ❍ Benevolent
C ❍ Principled
D ❍ Injurious

77 "Casting lots" seems like:
A ❍ Buying raw land
B ❍ Gambling
C ❍ Playing checkers
D ❍ Tossing sticks & stones

78 A Hebrew is the same as:
A ❍ One from beyond
B ❍ A male barista
C ❍ A foreigner in Canaan
D ❍ An Israelite

79 "Lord" is the same as:
A ❍ The One to whom I belong
B ❍ Czar
C ❍ Heathen deity
D ❍ The big guy

80 To be reverent is to be:
A ❍ Cheeky
B ❍ Impudent
C ❍ Respectful
D ❍ Submissive

81 Paraphrased text:
A ❍ Can add clarity
B ❍ Gives writers freedom
C ❍ Is not exact
D ❍ Can be a person's opinion

82 A natural tendency of mankind:
A ❍ Bow down
B ❍ Humility
C ❍ Pride
D ❍ Self-regard

83 One who is humble is:
A ❍ Able to subdue self
B ❍ Egotistical
C ❍ Arrogant
D ❍ Egocentric

84 God's will was determined by:
A ❍ Rolling the dice
B ❍ Drawing straws
C ❍ Flipping a coin
D ❍ Casting lots

85 Jonah was the:
A ❍ Odd man out
B ❍ Scapegoat
C ❍ Cause of the storm
D ❍ Perfect passenger

86 Jonah could have:
A ❍ Kept quiet
B ❍ Jumped ship
C ❍ Learned to swim
D ❍ Fought the sailors

87 Omniscience means:
A ❍ Unlimited power
B ❍ Unlimited presence
C ❍ Unlimited knowledge
D ❍ No awareness

88 Bible students should:
A ❍ Meditate
B ❍ Speculate
C ❍ Contemplate
D ❍ View different aspects

89 Jonah was:
A ❍ Mentally unwell
B ❍ A conflicted individual
C ❍ Suicidal
D ❍ Coo-coo crazy

90 Chaos is equal to:
A ❍ Fear
B ❍ Confusion
C ❍ Orderliness
D ❍ Balance

91 Solely regarding one's interest:
A ❍ Selfless
B ❍ Considerate
C ❍ Self-sacrificing
D ❍ Selfish

92 The Mediterranean Sea is:
A ❍ A small body of water
B ❍ About the size of Hawaii
C ❍ About half the size of USA
D ❍ Off the coast of Iceland

93 Agitation of mind to excite is:
A ❍ Emotion
B ❍ Intentional Emotion
C ❍ Feeling
D ❍ Passion

94 Violent means:
A ❍ Driven with force
B ❍ Vehement
C ❍ Outrageous
D ❍ Fierce

95 The word beseech means:
A ❍ Ah, I pray!
B ❍ Pray now!
C ❍ Oh may it be.
D ❍ Seech a bee

96 Jonah's testimony was:
A ❍ Bad
B ❍ Good
C ❍ Contradictory
D ❍ Hypocritical

97 In the Bible, blood can mean:
A ❍ Circulatory fluid in veins
B ❍ Bloodshed, slaughter
C ❍ Relatives by birth, marriage
D ❍ Gangs

98 Jonah is:
A ❍ A fool
B ❍ A priest
C ❍ A prophet
D ❍ A king

99 False prophets:
A ❍ Speak lies in God's name
B ❍ Have false vision
C ❍ Might practice witchcraft
D ❍ Tell information of no value

100 Diviners:
A ❍ Accurately foretell
B ❍ Guess
C ❍ Make predictions
D ❍ Are not inspired by God

101 A magician is the same as:
A ❍ Prophet
B ❍ Soothsayer
C ❍ Diviner
D ❍ Foreteller

102 These words go together:
A ❍ Iniquity & illegality
B ❍ Wicked & righteous
C ❍ Violation & iniquity
D ❍ Transgress & Trespass

103 Jesus' last name is:
A ❍ Anointed
B ❍ Christ
C ❍ Messiah
D ❍ Not mentioned

104 A false Christ is:
A ❍ Not legitimate
B ❍ Counterfeit
C ❍ A pretender
D ❍ Not of or from God

105 A seducer:
A ❍ Is faithful
B ❍ Goes out of the right way
C ❍ Leads from truth to error
D ❍ Tricks the simple-minded

106 A promise made:
A ❍ Binds the promise maker
B ❍ Is a declaration
C ❍ Is no big deal
D ❍ Should be taken seriously

107 To ordain means to:
A ❍ Set
B ❍ Establish
C ❍ Appoint
D ❍ Annul

108 To Believer's things happen by:
A ❍ Luck
B ❍ Chance
C ❍ Providence
D ❍ Coincidence

109 This is an animal:
A ❍ Fish
B ❍ Human
C ❍ Rock
D ❍ Worm

110 Fish are:
A ❍ Mammals
B ❍ Warm-blooded
C ❍ Not mammals
D ❍ Cold-blooded

111 A whale shark is:
A ❍ The largest shark
B ❍ Vicious
C ❍ The largest whale
D ❍ Docile

112 An Orca or Killer is:
A ❍ A medium-sized whale
B ❍ Toothless
C ❍ A dolphin
D ❍ Melon-headed

113 Whale are:
A ❍ Mammals
B ❍ Warm-blooded
C ❍ Not mammals
D ❍ Cold-blooded

114 Jonah was in the fish for:
A ❍ Three seconds
B ❍ Three minutes
C ❍ Three hours
D ❍ Three days

115 A miracle is:
A ❍ Impossible
B ❍ A wonderful thing
C ❍ A display of God's power
D ❍ Contrary to laws of nature

116 Strong driving conviction is:
A ❍ Emotion
B ❍ Intentional Emotion
C ❍ Feeling
D ❍ Passion

117 Lazarus was dead for:
- A ❍ Four seconds
- B ❍ Four minutes
- C ❍ Four hours
- D ❍ Four days

118 Resurrection means:
- A ❍ A rising again
- B ❍ Recovery to life from death
- C ❍ Revival from a coma
- D ❍ Unable to be revived

119 Evil, adulterous generations:
- A ❍ Seek after signs
- B ❍ Are something of the past
- C ❍ Describe my generation
- D ❍ Don't believe God

120 God's anointed messenger is:
- A ❍ Judas
- B ❍ Joses
- C ❍ Jezebel
- D ❍ Jesus

121 Inquisitive students seek:
- A ❍ Information by questions
- B ❍ Knowledge and discussion
- C ❍ To prove what they believe
- D ❍ Believe everything and one

122 Jonah was resurrected:
- A ❍ Yes
- B ❍ No
- C ❍ Possibly
- D ❍ There's no way to know

123 This isn't accurate:
- A ❍ Jesus alone in a boat
- B ❍ Jonah jumping off a boat
- C ❍ Jonah alone in a boat
- D ❍ Jonah walking on water

124 I am accountable to:
- A ❍ Jesus
- B ❍ My Creator, Maker, God
- C ❍ The Holy Spirit
- D ❍ No one

125 The account of Jonah is:
- A ❍ Fiction
- B ❍ Non-fiction
- C ❍ Maybe both
- D ❍ I don't know

126 My opinion on amplified text:
- A ❍ Helpful
- B ❍ Learned to like it
- C ❍ Annoying
- D ❍ Leaves little to no doubt

127 In this study, I learned:
- A ❍ A lot
- B ❍ Very little
- C ❍ Nothing new
- D ❍ Some things

Lastly: "The Final Exam" ➜

Pass it and you're good for life!

The Final Exam

God with _ _

Isaiah 7:14 **Therefore the Lord himself shall give you a sign; Behold, a virgin shall conceive, and bear a son, and shall call his name Immanuel** [God with us; the prophetic name of the Messiah, the Christ]**.**

He shall _ _ _ _ his people from their _ _ _ _

Matthew 1:21 **And she shall bring forth a son, and you shall call his name JESUS:** [the Son of God, the Savior of mankind] **for he shall save his people from their sins.**

_ _ _ _ iniquities And your _ _ _ _ ...

Isaiah 59:2 **But your iniquities** [crimes; guilt] **have made a separation between you and your God, And your sins** [offenses against God and man] **have hidden His face from you so that He does not hear.**

be zealous therefore, and _ _ _ _ _ _

Revelation 3:19–20 **As many as I love, I rebuke** [find fault with; correct] **and chasten:** [discipline] **be zealous therefore, and repent.** [change your mind; feel remorse from a consciousness of guilt]
20 **Behold, I stand at the door, and knock: if any man hear my voice, and open the door, I will come in to him, and will sup with him, and he with me.**

If we _ _ _ _ _ _ _

1 John 1:9 **If we confess** [declare openly; not deny] **our sins, He is faithful and righteous to forgive us our sins and to cleanse us from all unrighteousness.**

You _ _ _ _ be born _ _ _ _ _

John 3:1–7 *1* **There was a man of the Pharisees, named Nicodemus, a ruler of the Jews:** *2* **The same came to Jesus by night, and said to him, Rabbi, we know that you are a teacher come from God: for no man can do these miracles that you do, except God be with him.** *3* **Jesus answered and said to him, Verily, verily, I say to you, Except a man be born again, he cannot see the kingdom of God.** *4* **Nicodemus said to him, How can a man be born when he is old? can he enter the second time into his mother's womb, and be born?** *5***Jesus answered, Verily, verily, I say to you, Except a man be born of water and of the Spirit, he cannot enter into the kingdom of God.** *6* **That which is born of the flesh is flesh; and that which is born of the Spirit is spirit.** *7* **Marvel not that I said to you, You must be born again.**

He that _ _ _ _ _ _ _ _ _ _

John 3:16 **For God so loved the world, that he gave his only begotten Son, that whoever believes in him should not perish, but have everlasting life.** *17* **For God sent not his Son into the world to condemn the world; but that the world through him might be saved.** *18* **He that believes on him is not condemned: but he that believes not is condemned already, because he has not believed in the name of the only begotten Son of God.**

Give ear, O Lord, to my _ _ _ _ _ _ _

Psalm 86:5–7 **For you, Lord, are good, and ready to forgive; and plenteous in mercy to all them that call upon you.** *6* **Give ear, O Lord, to my prayer; and attend to the voice of my supplications.** *7* **In the day of my trouble I will call upon thee: for thou wilt answer me.**

you _ _ _ _ _ be _ _ _ _ _ _

Romans 10:9 **that if you confess with your mouth Jesus as Lord,** [supreme in authority] **and believe in your heart that God raised Him from the dead, you will be saved;**

Every one that asks _ _ _ _ _ _ _ _ _ _

Matthew 7:7–8 *7* **Ask, and it shall be given you; seek, and you shall find; knock, and it shall be opened to you:** *8* **For every one that asks receives; and he that seeks finds; and to him that knocks it shall be opened.**

Who is Lord of your life? You decide.

Here is a sample prayer:

God, I'm wrong—you're right.

I am guilty of breaking your commandments. Please forgive me of all offenses against You and others.

I believe you were crucified and died for me which paid the penalty of my sins. You are my Savior.

I agree with your word that I need to be born of the Spirit—born again. I surrender my will to Yours.
I accept you as Lord of my life.

I need help to live by Your standards. Fill me with your Holy Spirit. Speak to me as I read the Bible.

Thank you for the promise of everlasting life, and for hearing and answering this prayer, in the name of Jesus, Amen.

This type of prayer is answered *immediately*. The words won't save you, but if your heart is sincere, you have become a Christian.

According to John 3:5-7, I am born again. ❍True ❍False ❍?

This is my born again spiritual birth date: __/__/____

www.ingramcontent.com/pod-product-compliance
Lightning Source LLC
Chambersburg PA
CBHW081324090426
42737CB00017B/3022

9781639420452